MW01628781

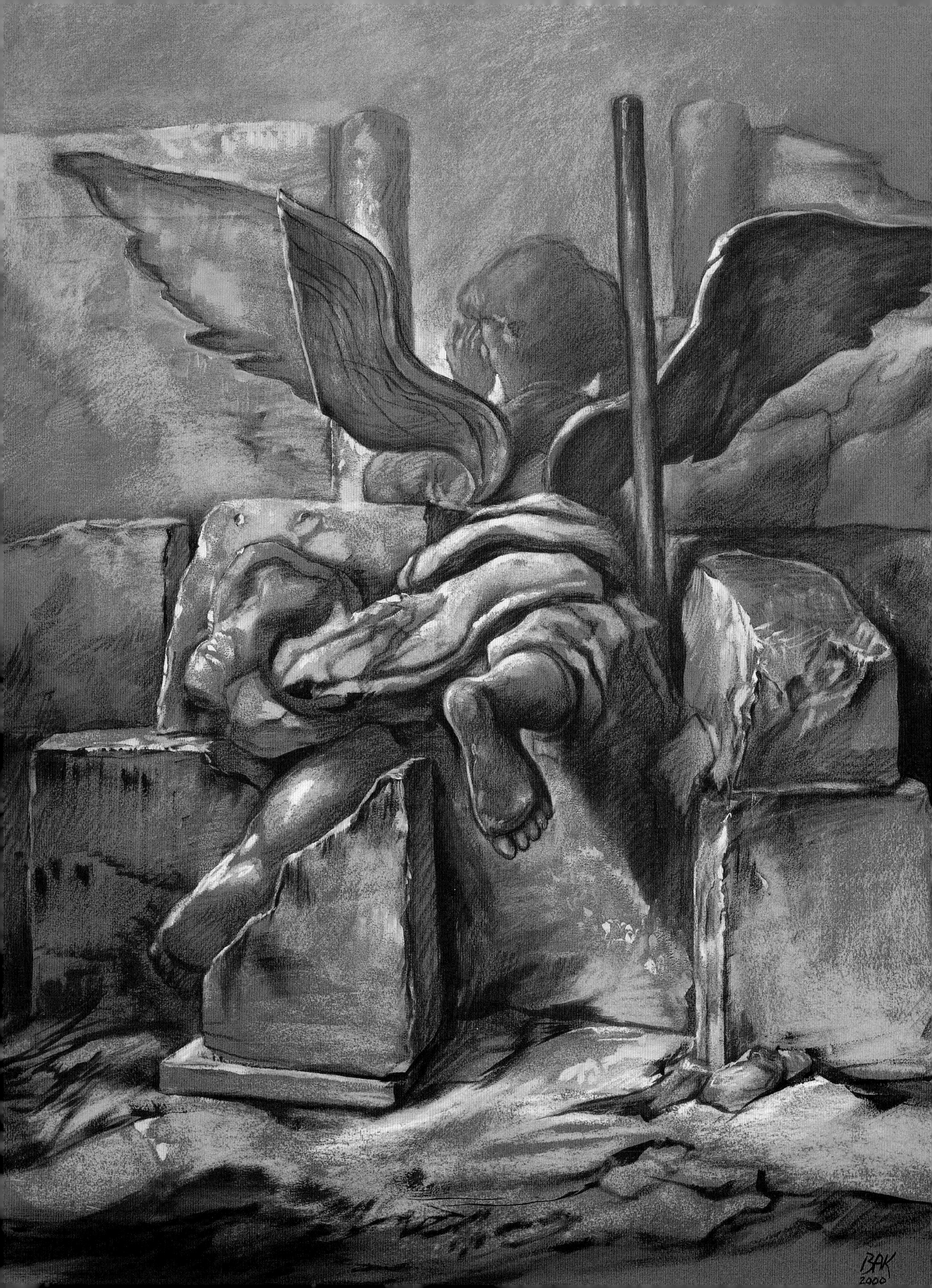
BAK
2000

IN A DIFFERENT LIGHT

Rembrandt's Angel, 2000
Crayon & oil on brown paper, 25 1/2 x 19 3/4"

Credits
Editor: Jeanne Gressler
Photography: Max Coniglio

Library of Congress Cataloging-in-Publication Data

Langer, Lawrence L.
In a different light : genesis in the art of Samuel Bak / Lawrence L.
Langer.
p. cm.
ISBN 1-879985-06-3
1. Bak, Samuel--Themes, motives. I. Bak, Samuel. II. Title.
N7279.B24 A4 2001
759.95694--dc21
2001000838

Pucker Gallery
171 Newbury Street
Boston, MA 02116
(617) 267-9473
(617) 424-9759 fax
www.puckergallery.com
contactus@puckergallery.com

Distributed by University of Washington Press
P.O. Box 50096
Seattle, WA 98145-5096

With special thanks to Irene Tayler for her editorial help with My Mother's Bereyshiss.

IN A DIFFERENT LIGHT

The Book of Genesis in the Art of Samuel Bak

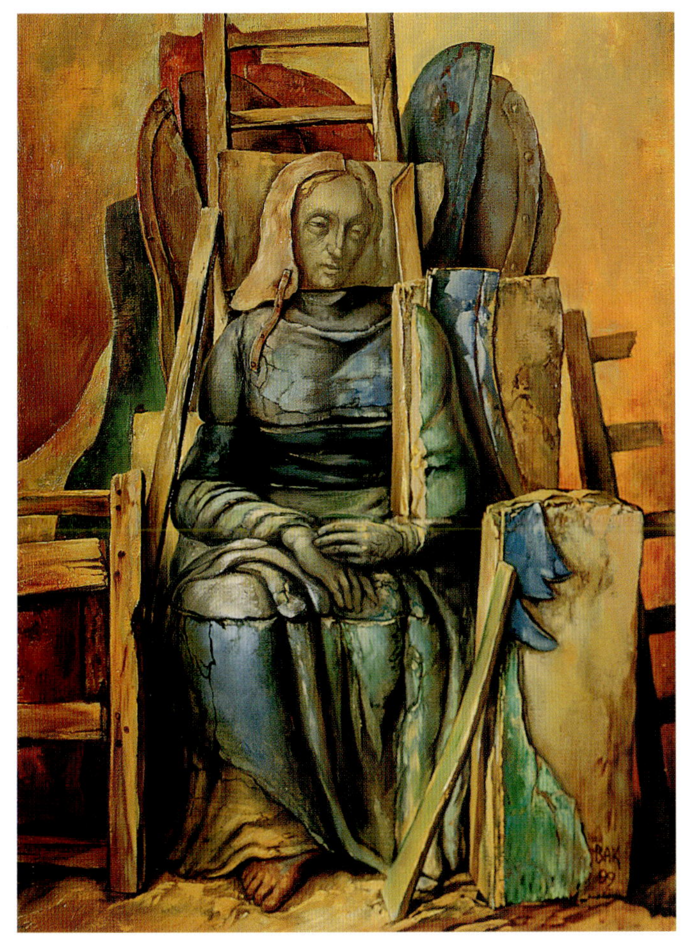

Study for Rainbow Angel, 1999
Oil on canvas, 16 x 12"

Lawrence L. Langer

Post script by Samuel Bak

My Mother's *Bereyshiss*

The Book of Genesis begins with the creation of the world and its first human occupants and ends with the death of Jacob, the last of the patriarchs. A brief coda, the closing words of the narrative announce the death of Joseph: "and they embalmed him and he was put in a coffin in Egypt." But this is not necessarily a melancholy image, since it prepares the reader for the Book of Exodus where Moses will lead the Jewish people out of bondage on a journey through the desert toward a Promised Land. The Torah ends with the death of Moses, but here again the passing of a great leader is only the harbinger of a more expansive future.

This, however, is only one strain of a multi-layered story. Scarcely has Genesis begun when an act of disobedience shatters the infinitude of the initial creation and girdles time with the stricture of mortality. Soon after, fraternal rivalry initiates a pattern of violence that will become a defining feature of human history. One of the first inquiries in Hebrew Scripture is: "Where is thy brother Abel?" to which Cain replies: "I do not know. Am I my brother's keeper?" That question echoes through the centuries to a peace-seeking civilization still groping for an appropriate response. The ending of Genesis provides a temporary answer, as Joseph is reconciled with his brothers when he responds generously to their plea for forgiveness. It is one of the many instances of *tikkun*, of healing or repair, which threads through the writings comprising the Jewish Testament. But other events within and beyond Scripture reveal the limited stamina of such a feat, confirming the necessity to reprise it through the ages.

In an essay called "Tradition and the Individual Talent," T.S.

Eliot wrote of the duty to reconsider past literature in the light of later ideas that could not have been predicted by the original artists. The advent of Freud, for example, created an opportunity for new insights that ordained a revising of the critical legacy. Similarly, in his recent cycle of paintings and drawings, *In a Different Light*, Samuel Bak has shaped a visual universe of discourse that reviews the assumptions of Genesis through the revelations of a later "text" called the Book of the Holocaust – canonically impossible, of course, but intellectually plausible and indeed, in its influence on his work, a source of major imaginative vitality. Bak is not the first artist to note the impact of the involuntary modern voyage of the children of Israel from life to death on prior accounts of the Jewish journey into and back from exile. But he is one of very few to focus so persistently on the importance of this theme. As a result of the Holocaust, a radical shift in thinking about the meaning of covenant has emerged, reducing the nostalgia for a simple renewal of belief to a minor key. In a sense, Bak redraws the lines between man and God, Adam and his Creator, human dreams and divine purpose, time and eternity, the whole spiritual drama that inspires the most crucial moments of Hebrew Scripture. *Genesis* contains several instances of the suspension of divine compassion following human mutiny. But even more constant is the motif of divine assurance to the Chosen People of protection from their enemies. To the eye of the contemporary reader, however, a sinister irony pervades the imagery surrounding that promise in the closing lines of the Book of Malachi, the last of the prophets, whose words in the King James version are also among the final ones of the entire Old Testament as prepared for a Christian audience: "For lo! That day is at hand, burning like an oven. All the arrogant and all the doers of evil shall be straw, and the day that is coming – said the Lord of Hosts – shall burn them to ashes." When a prophecy designed to comfort ended up confusing the righteous with the wicked, when an innocent use of oven and ashes upset the moral balance, in Malachi's language, for "those who revere the Lord and esteem His name," then the Jewish self was obliged to reexamine its identity and the bond that joined it to an ancient and honorable religious tradition.

Samuel Bak has chosen a return to beginnings as his point

of departure in the series called *In a Different Light*. He imprints on the original template of Creation signs of disarray that stain the purity of the pristine scene. Bak literally adopts Eliot's injunction to re-view the work of early masters through the vista of later intellectual and spiritual history by turning to the most monumental representation of *Genesis* in the annals of art, Michelangelo's paintings on the ceiling of the Sistine Chapel. Bak's idea itself is a *tour de force*, since art has long played a principal role in shaping our concept of our fate. In a bold imaginative stroke he redesigns the foremost visual text of the Creation, deconstructs its fixed features and recasts them through the eyes of modernity. Present consciousness requires efforts like these if we are to see clearly the damage done by the ravages of history to standard representations of our numinous past and future. Michelangelo himself adapted a story from Hebrew Scripture to Christianity's vision of the human journey from Creation to the Last Judgment. Visitors to the Sistine Chapel can take in the majestic sweep of this quintessential voyage and the sublime hierarchy implicit in its artistic depiction. Despite the rivalries and conflicts of the early Renaissance, an age of faith saw no reason to question the supremacy of that hierarchy.

But Bak's personal history, together with his evolving artistic growth, furnished many reasons for questioning the assumptions behind both scriptural and Renaissance views of the Creation. For the familiar consolation of extracting hope for redemption from various channels of despair he substitutes the task of inquiring into the possibilities and impossibilities of reestablishing a meaningful covenant with its original Author. This in turn might illuminate the uncertain destiny of that agreement without ignoring the events that had questioned its sanctity. Such doubts rarely entered the minds of the earliest visitors to the Sistine Chapel. The structure of the place reinforced the heavenly hierarchy that defined religious belief of the time. Even today, viewers of the ceiling cannot escape the lofty sensation of having the gaze swept upward to confront the prodigious spectacle of what one Michelangelo scholar has called a "metaphor of the universal order and of a fixed and immutable divine design."

When the visual examination of the vast space above finally ends and the line of sight resumes its horizontal vector, it is greeted by the equally colossal *Last Judgment.* In this encounter with the spiritual design of the universe, the division between heavenly and earthly zones affirms the preordained journey of the soul from birth to eternity. For these orthodox options of blessing and damnation Bak substitutes a cyclic view of experience, an alternation between creative action and ruin that is embodied in the imagery and spatial design of his paintings. They reflect the process of redefining the role of the human creature within the framework of modern existence. The troubling questions Bak raises may not be new, but the moral energy behind his inquiries emerges through a highly original metaphorical vision. If the universe was once God's temple and man and woman its noblest inhabitants, what has happened to the splendor of the primordial conception? Viewed "in a different light," through the lens of history, the purer purposes of eternity seem constantly to have been thwarted by the bloody plunders of time. Such a conflict establishes in the story of the children of Israel an oscillation between exile and return, estrangement from and renewed intimacy with a Deity whose own position in the affairs of His people appears to vacillate between intimacy and default. To capture this dilemma on canvas is one of the major goals of Samuel Bak's new sequence of drawings and paintings. If according to the artist's view the Holocaust has left us a legacy of Jewish memory in a state of disrepair, the image of the God of the Hebrews has suffered some damages too.

Michelangelo would have been dismayed by the trend of this argument. For him, the honor of mankind lay in heeding and enacting the intentions of divine will. The Sistine Ceiling portrays the newly created Adam and Eve as figures of perfect comeliness and grace. Their distorted features after the expulsion result from a human breach for which their Creator bears no responsibility. Michelangelo's God as He separates light from darkness is an anthropomorphic agent of awesome power whose patriarchal bearing differs sharply from the silhouettes of vacancy with which Bak chooses to replace Him in his various emendations of the Creation of Adam. In his *Life of Michelangelo* Vasari had called the Adam of the original Sistine painting "a figure whose beauty, pose, and contours are such that it seems to have been fashioned that very moment by the first and supreme Creator rather than by the drawing and brush of a mortal man." Bak's blueprints for Adam acknowledge the impossibility of duplicating the chaste gleaming flesh of his model in a post-Holocaust era that has seen so much violation of the body. Any effort to restore its unsullied status would be a naïve expression of nostalgic yearning, a sacrilege against the anguish of time.

Michelangelo's *Creation of Adam* is charged with tension between human expectation and divine wish. The focal point is the narrow space dividing God's resolute finger from Adam's languid hand, awaiting the spark of vitality that will give it life. The symmetrical skill that separates God in a regal purple cloak from a naked Adam highlights the one-way transmission of energy from omnipotent divine source to inert human dependent. God's rigid digit is about to animate the flaccid finger of Adam, whose latent virility is proclaimed by the sculptured muscularity of his flesh. If we turn now to Bak's *Adam and Eve*, we discover a composition that accents a changed pictorial reality, based not on the inviolable hierarchical principles enshrined in Scripture but on the disrupted continuum entombed in history. The monochromatic tones of the painting, more fiery than bleak, barely distinguish its human figures from the surrounding landscape. A forlorn and weary-eyed Adam resembles the last Jew more than the first Man as he leans in the shadow of a massive brick structure which those familiar with Bak's earlier work will instantly recognize as the wall from a chamber of death. Its solid substance frames and almost visually consumes the thinly outlined profile of Michelangelo's Deity, His former power seemingly sapped by the looming edifice behind him. From a rent in God's cloak, which is also a breach in the chamber wall, peers the sorrowful face of a post-Holocaust Eve, whether victim or survivor we have no way of knowing. Does Adam mourn her loss, or await her return? The principal activity in the canvas is pointing, but the hands represent a trio of skeptical gestures that promise neither union nor even touch. Eve points toward Adam, who does not

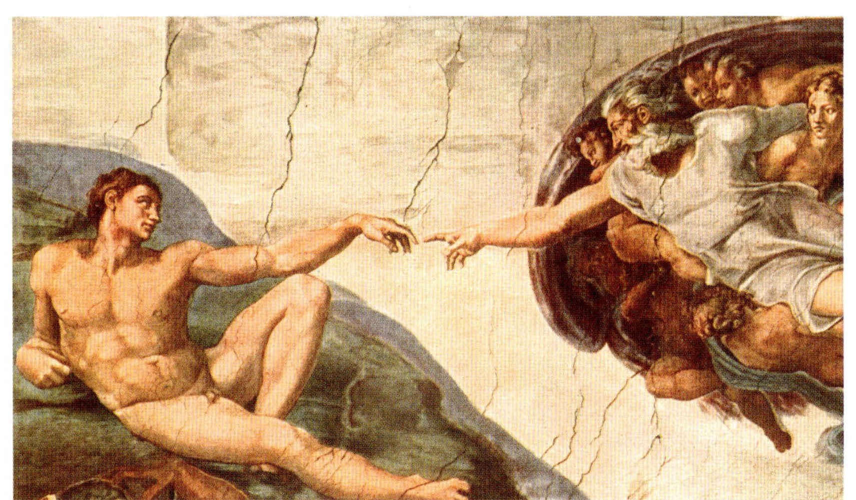

Michelangelo's *Creation of Adam*

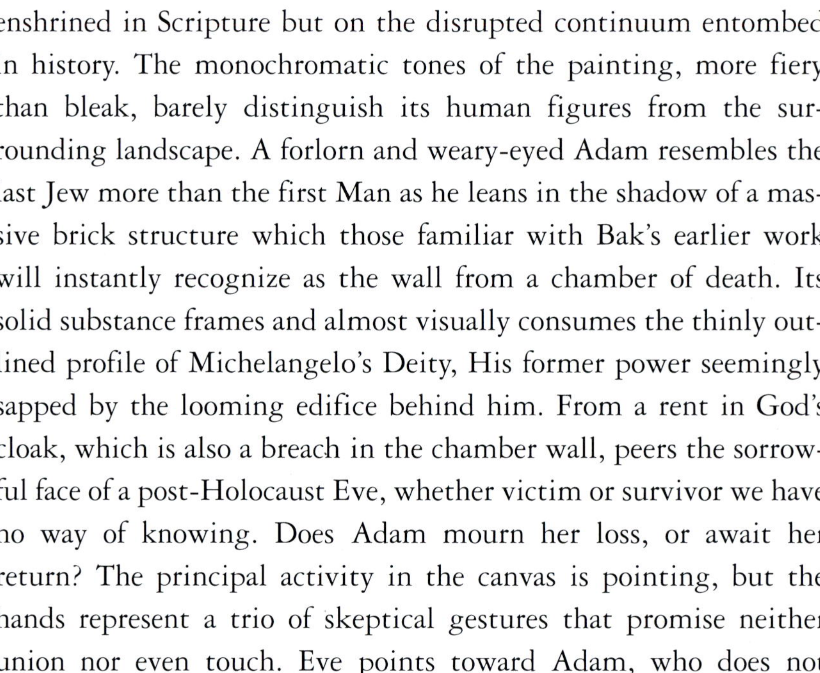

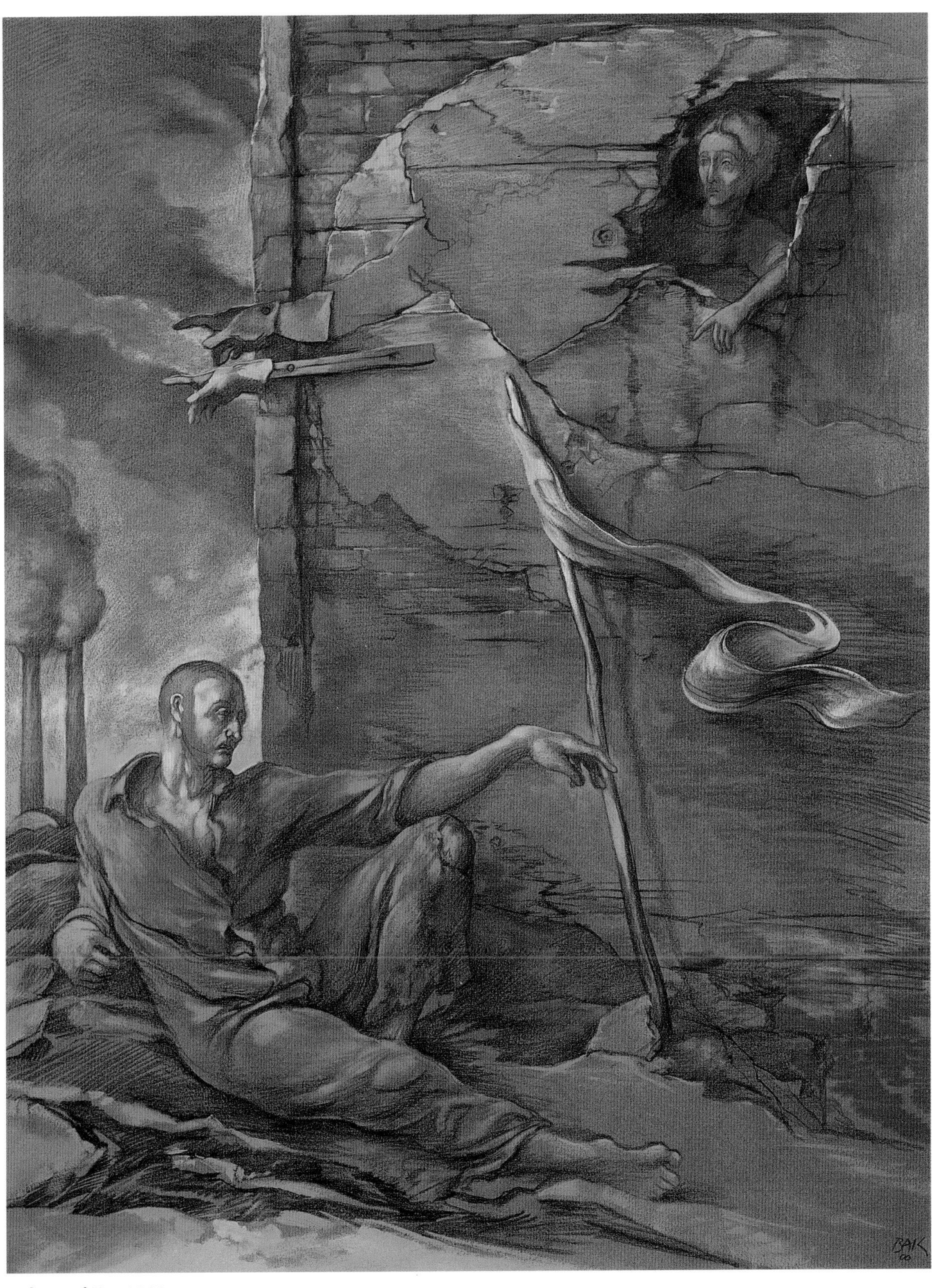

Adam and Eve, 2000
Crayon & oil on brown paper, 25 1/2 x 19 3/4"

return her gaze. The hand of God has lost its way; its finger aims not at Adam but at a distant object in the vicinity of twin crematorium chimneys. When God said "Let there be light," did He foresee the ghastly illumination from these flames of death? The observer is left with the challenge of fusing in the imagination the Holocaust story of uncreation with the dazzling instant of human origin portrayed by Michelangelo.

Adam and Eve also prepares us for the ironic merger of sacred and profane narratives that will be a fundamental strategy of many of the paintings from *In a Different Light*. Several metaphors for the idea of divine guidance gone astray vie for our attention in these canvases. Because it was forbidden to look upon God's countenance, a pillar of smoke guided the children of Israel on their journey through the desert. In *Adam and Eve* (and most other variations in the "creation" group) two columns appear as surrogate signs not of a journey to freedom but of a voyage to death. The finger of God points in their direction, but whether to hurl a divine "J'accuse" at those who have corrupted His plan or as a post-mortem decision to include a different kind of darkness in the original design, the distressed viewer is left to decipher. Adding to the interpretive dilemma is the unmistakable image of God's hand crossing a ridge of bricks in a cruciform motion. As if to confirm the artist's intent, just beneath it a gloved piece of wood in the form of a hand is nailed to the brick façade. It is a fixed sign of the need to seek new meaning and guidance after the failure of the Christian doctrine of mercy and forgiveness to forestall the destruction of European Jewry.

All of this is part of the retinal audacity informing the works included in *In a Different Light*. They push our preconditioned eyes to see images other than they were trained to do by established versions of reality. Bak's frequent violation of familiar visual truth finally forces us to reconsider our memories of the historical and spiritual past and the systems of belief that were allied to them. As a result of the Holocaust, the unnatural has displaced much of the supernatural in its impact on modern consciousness. The artist Francis Bacon has said that a painter "has to capture not only the look of things but the emotions they arouse." Bak might add to this advice the corollary that sometimes a painter must undo the look of things in order to discredit the emotions they arouse, so

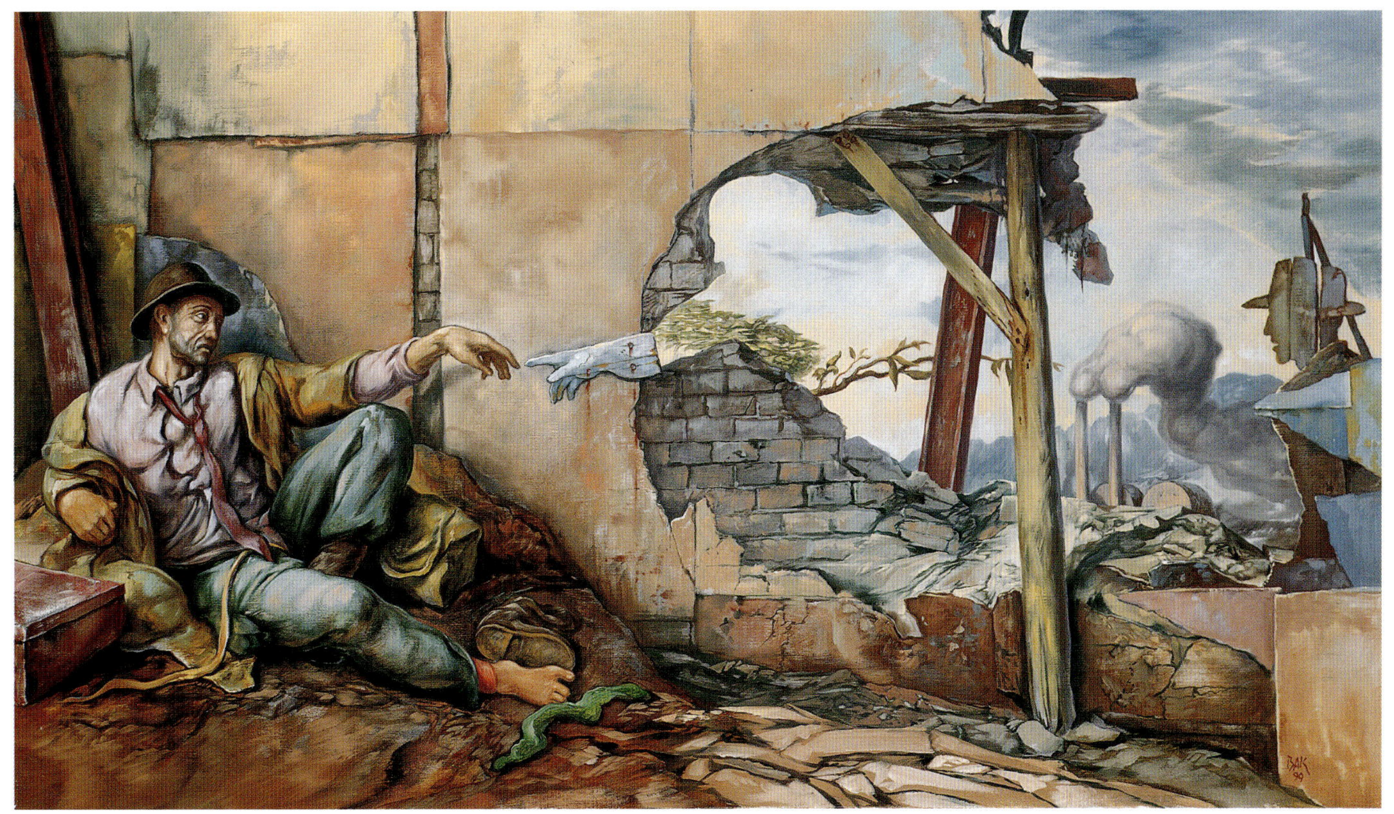

Creation of War Time, 1999
Oil on canvas, 32 x 40"

that more valid feelings may infiltrate the vacated space left by outmoded emotions. Bacon, who once defined man as a potential carcass, continued "I believe that realism has to be re-invented...This is the only possible way the painter can bring back the intensity of the reality he is trying to capture." Since the Holocaust was unknown to Michelangelo and undreamt of in his perception of reality, Bak had to find a kind of realism that would allow him to imprint on the archetypal version of Creation clues to that destruction. This in turn would substantially modify our response to Renaissance and other prior visions of human destiny.

Creation of War Time repeats the confrontation between Adam and God, but here God is even less defined, a cutout from the empty space that surrounds His image. A helmeted Adam leans upon a landscape in ruins, the tatters of his rainbow-colored garments summoning up memories of an ancient broken promise from biblical times. In the distance rise the familiar ominous pillars of smoke, haunting the foreground with their echoes of annihilation, while just behind them the curved tops of the Tablets of the Law peek furtively over a low ridge of stone. What fresh covenant will

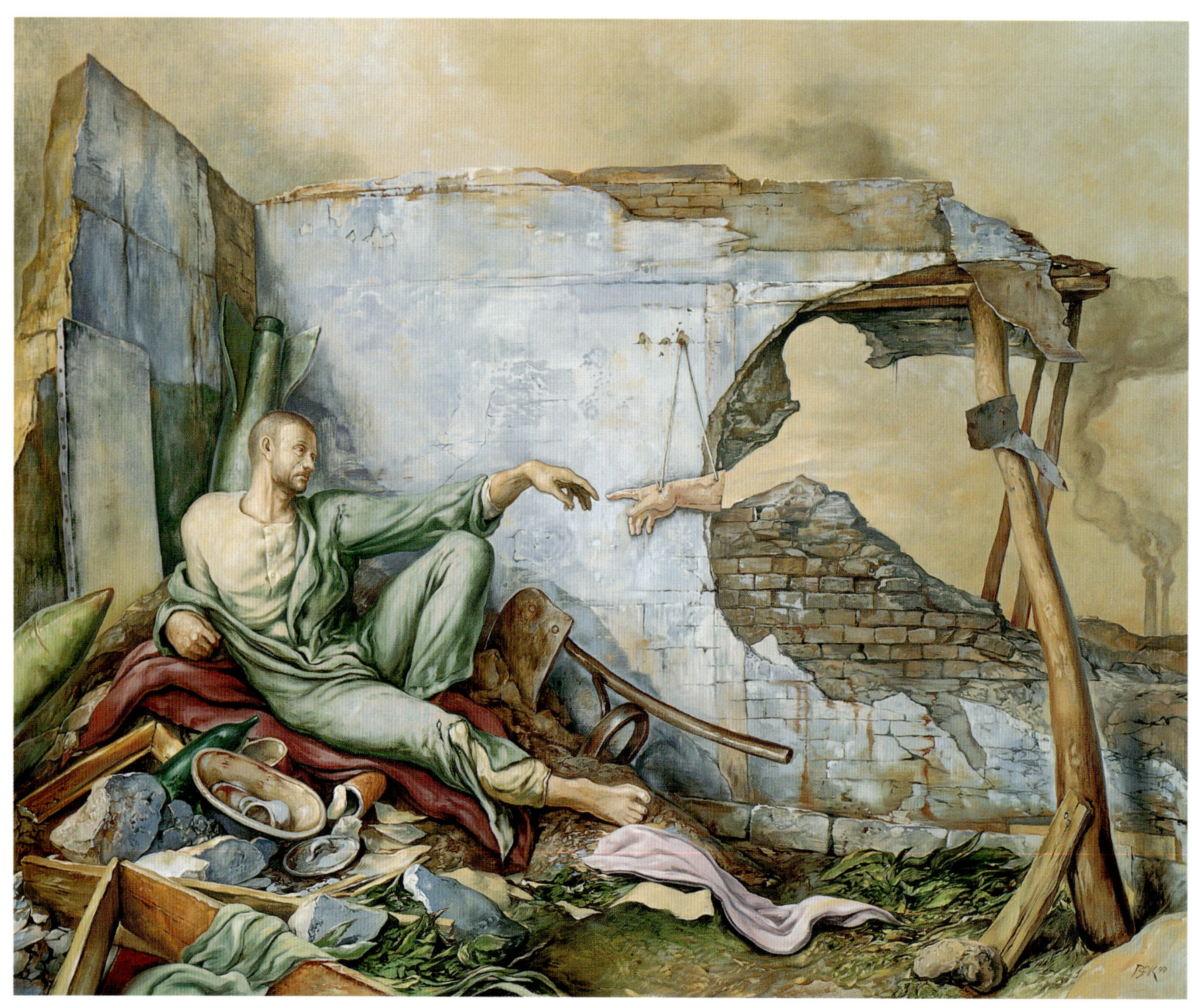

Creation of War Time, II, 1999
Oil on canvas, 32 x 40"

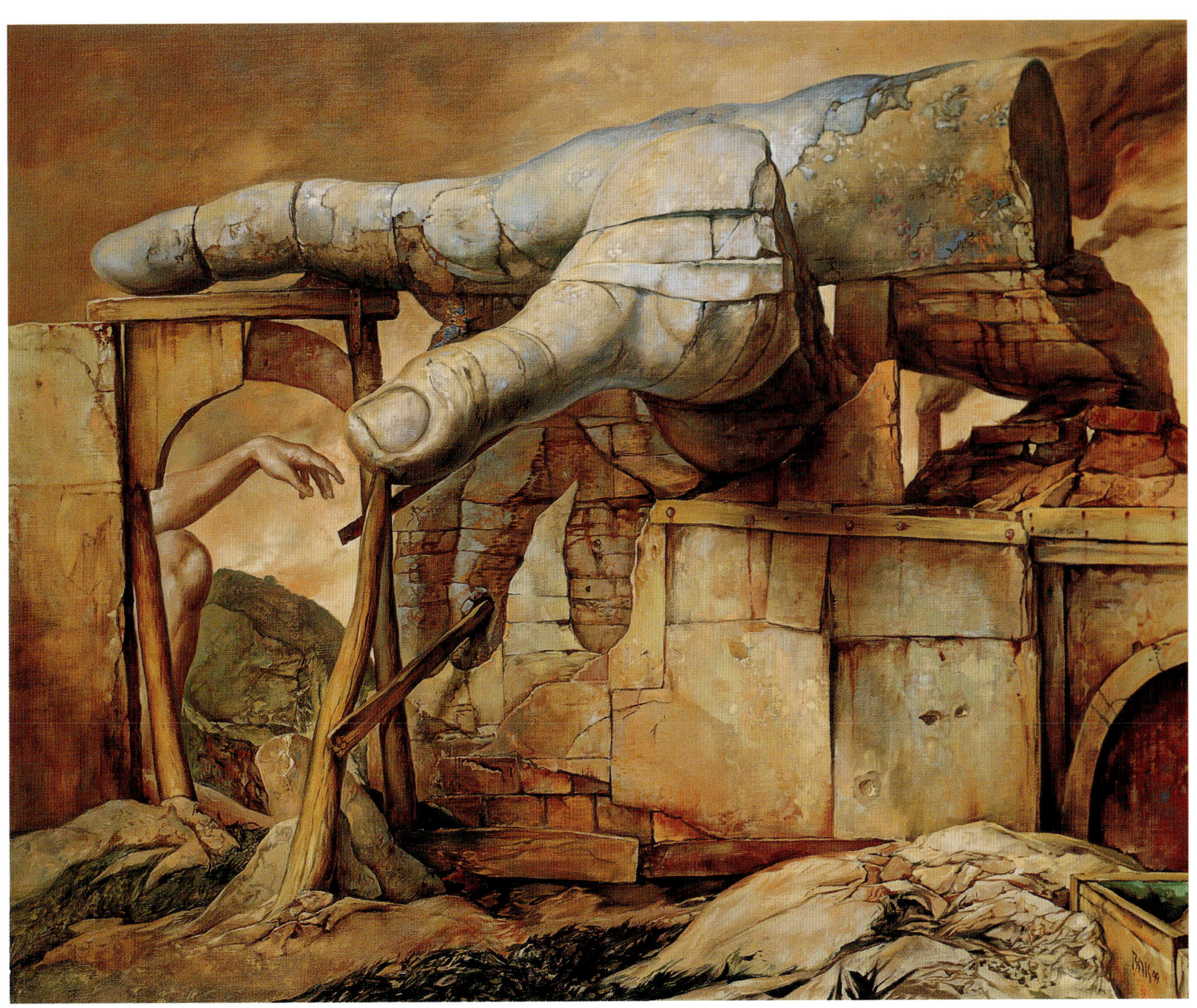

Open Door, 1999
Oil on canvas, 26 x 32"

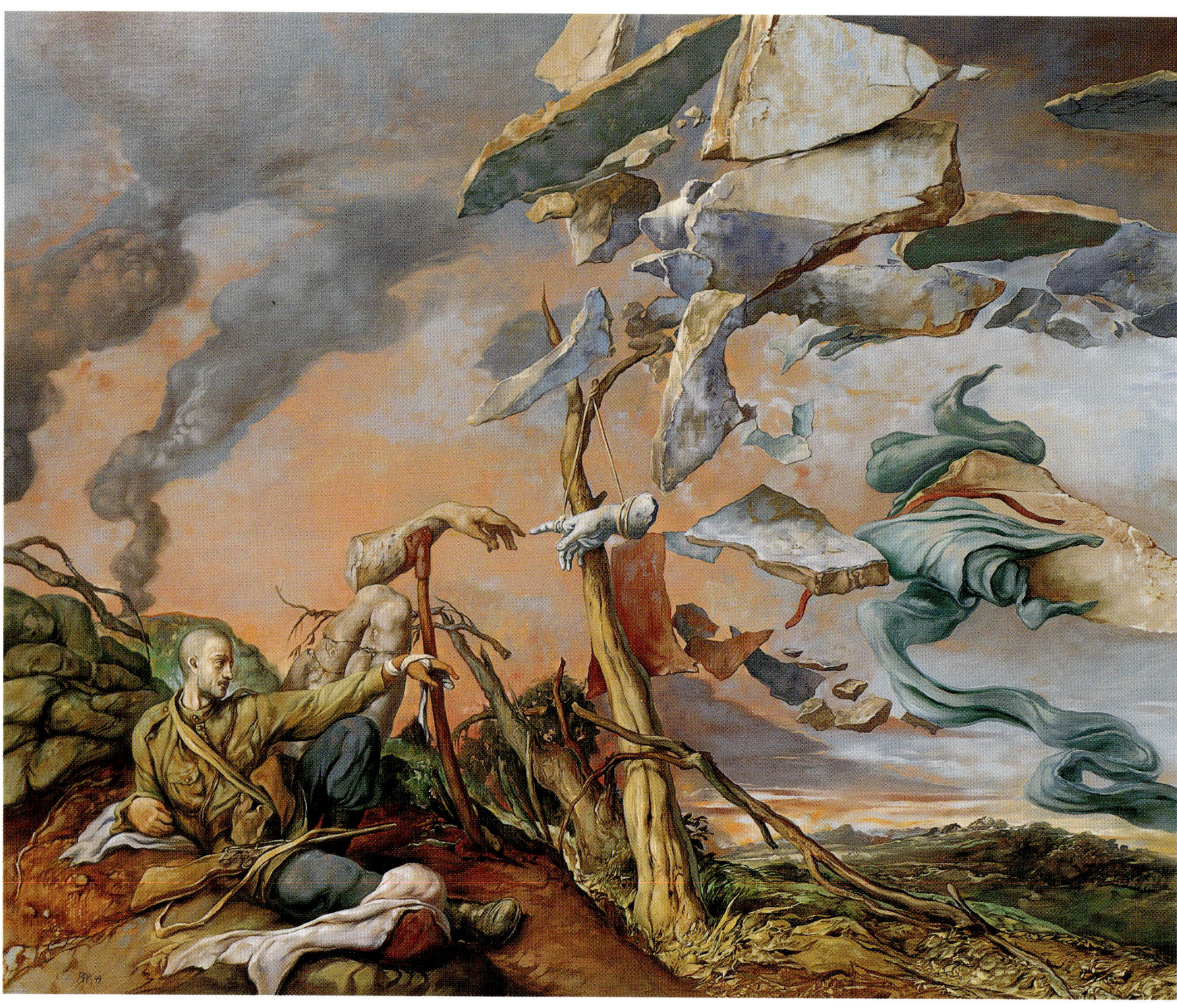

Creation, 1999
Oil on canvas, 40 x 50"

Creation, (detail)

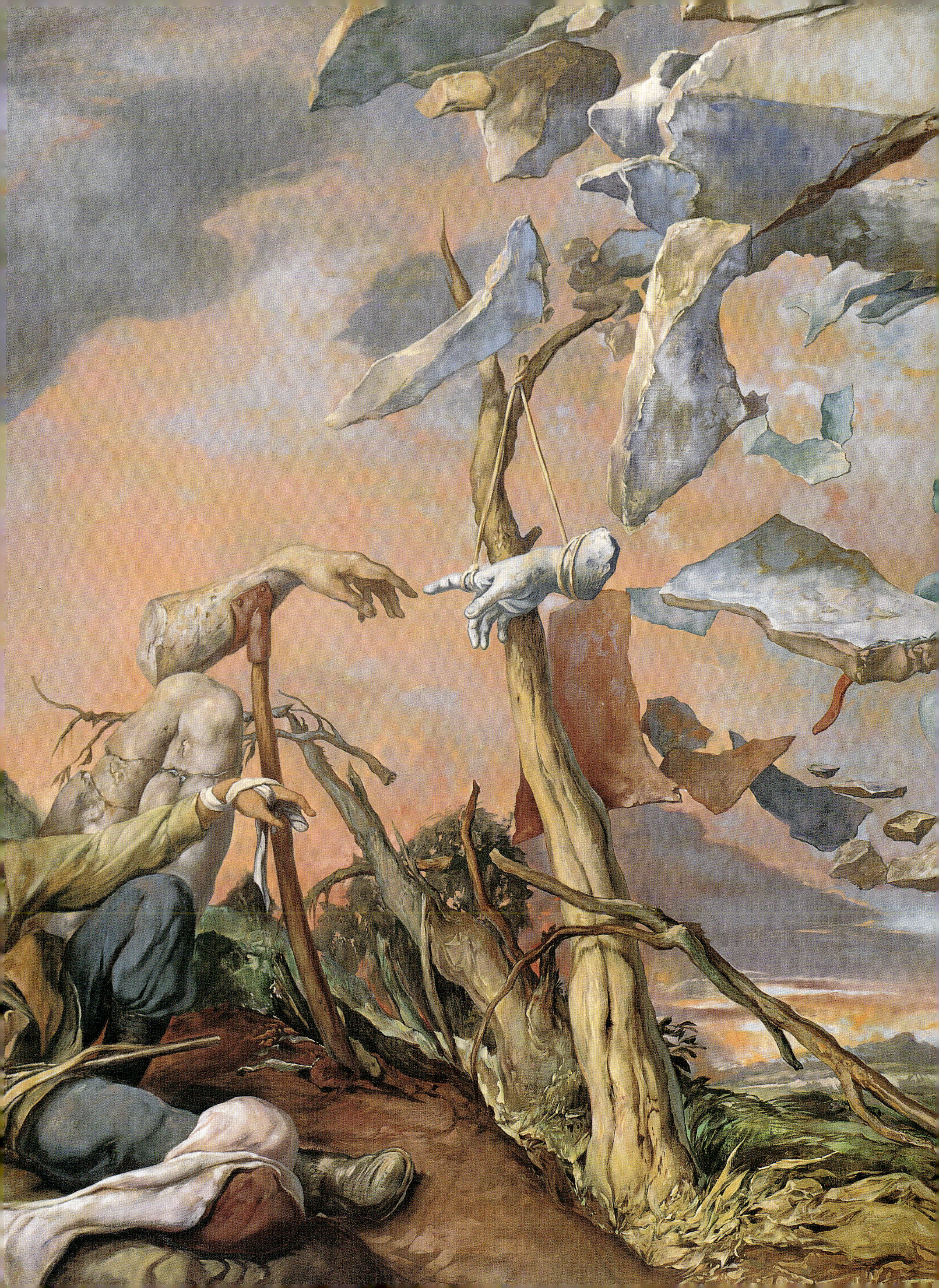

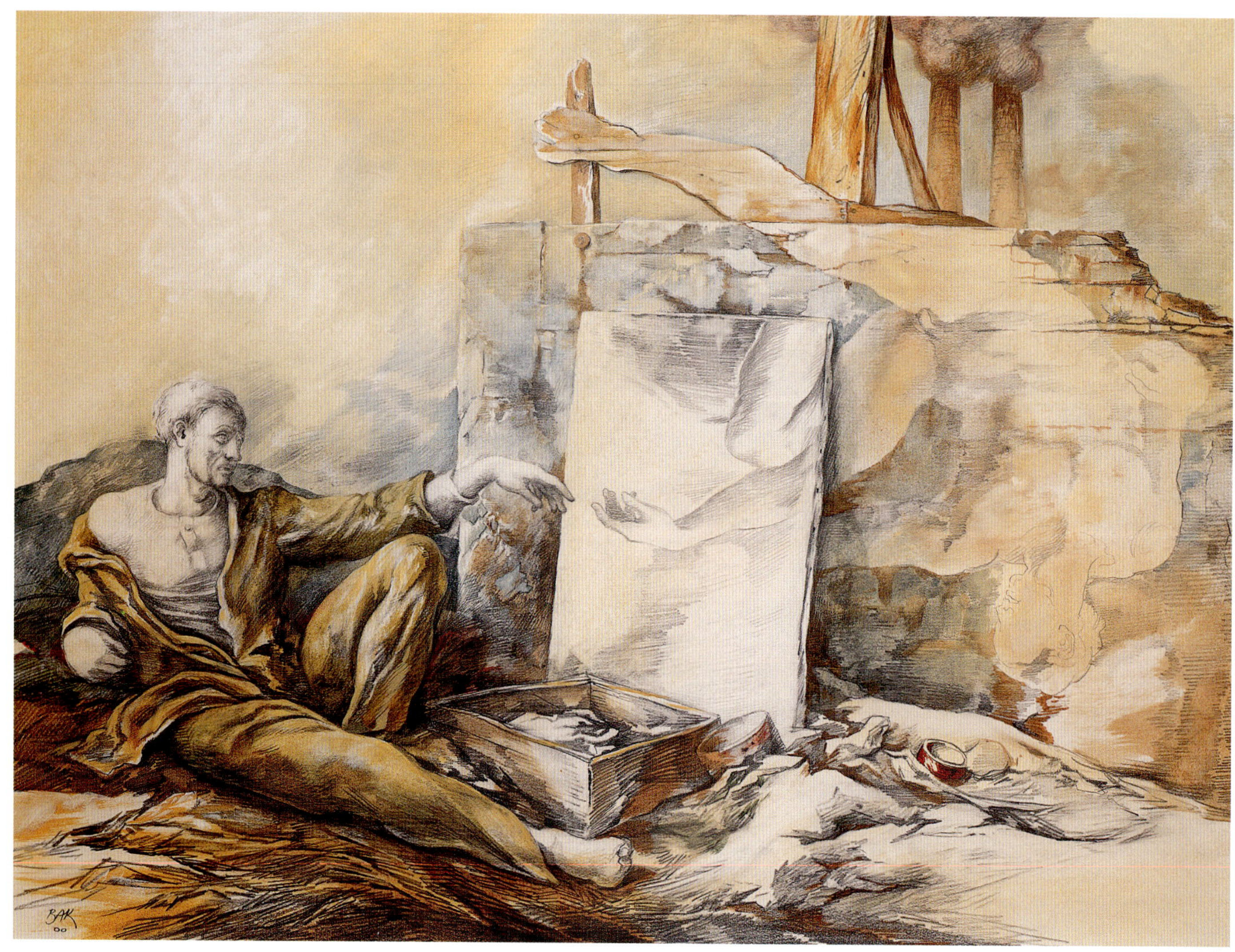

Adam with his own Image, 2000
Pencil & oil on paper, 22 x 30"

spring from the ravages of war and Holocaust? The sole sign of renewal is the tree that emerges from the silhouette of God's forearm. But the wary spectator will also note that it is adjacent to His hand, nailed to the wall while blood drips from a different kind of stigmata, leaving us with the disturbing facsimile of a wounded God. Both the painting and its images are inspired by times of violence that form a major legacy to the modern mind. Any renewal or return to creative vigor must be born from the arduous passage through Bak's fragmented landscapes of devastation.

One of the options in the group of creation paintings is to eliminate the figure of God and to leave Adam and the viewer to cope with His temporary disappearance. This is consistent with the view of the Holocaust as a story of the spiritual solitude of Jewish identity on its unwished for journey to an unpromised land. Variations like *Open Door* and *Adam with his own Image* violate the symmetry of Michelangelo's model by eliminating half of the cosmic design – the presence of God. In *Open Door** Adam is largely concealed, though his forearm, hand, and knee are vividly sculpted from human flesh. But God is totally absent, replaced by a huge installation of a hand composed of rusted metal and segmented stone, a hollow artifact that is detached from any divine source. In an ironic reversal, the tip of its thumb seems to gain some mortal substance from its proximity to Adam's finger, as if God were now to be remade in the image of man. But there appears to be little prospect for that here, as the giant hand dominates the painting's space as if to crush its content with its massive and monumental weight. What chance will the hidden Adam have to emerge unscathed? Against the symmetrical balance of Michelangelo's vision Bak has inserted an incompatible opposition, leaving the viewer wondering whether the "open door" is a place of exit or of entry. In the nineteenth century Nietzsche might have viewed this painting as a sign of the loss of contact between the human and the divine, as a hint of the abdication of God, as proof that the fully human could develop only after the withdrawal of divinity from the formation of the natural self. This may be further than Bak is willing to take us, but the imbalance between hands in *Open Door* certainly suggests that Adam may have to seek elsewhere for a reciprocal source of compassion.

**page 11*

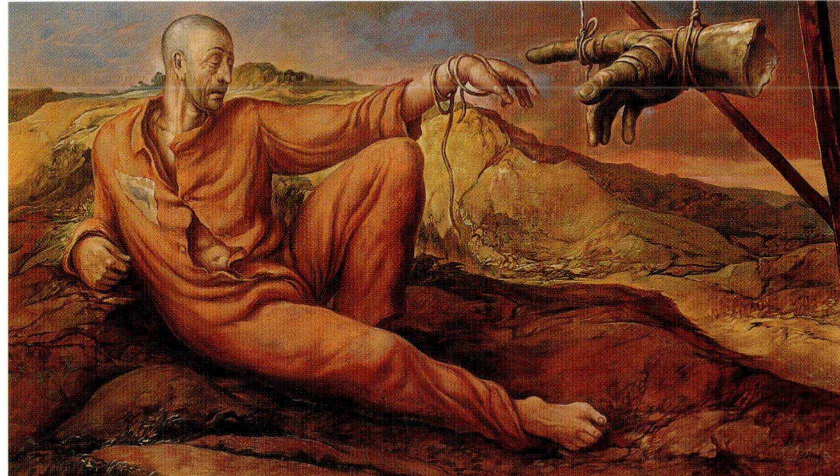

Joseph's Dream, 1999
Oil on canvas, 18 x 32"

*page 14

One is at least invited to contemplate such a likelihood in *Adam with his own Image**, where a reclining Adam sculpted from stone but clothed in human garments faces an inverted reflection of himself. Does this signify that after the Holocaust, whose signature chimneys menace the landscape, man is obliged to recreate himself in his *own* image? Is it an endorsement of solipsism, the notion that man can know only himself, or a meditation on the narcissistic impulse, a fatal habit in myth and a hint of vanity in Milton's Eve? It is a question for art as well as philosophy, as the marble Adam indicates. It would take the ingenuity of a modern Michelangelo to carve from the block of stone containing Adam's reflection a human shape consistent with the anguish it has survived. For the artist representation precedes understanding; the large slab before Adam seems to have fallen from the easel behind the block of stone, and in order to transmute himself from marble into flesh, the hand of Adam, or one of his human descendants, will have to become its own instrument of creation.

Without some form of self-definition, the Adam of *Searching* is on the verge of collapsing into a crumbling ruin. Severed hands of wood and stone are pointing in opposite directions, propped up by artificial supports that are detached from any vital source, human or divine. Archeologists of the future will excavate this terrain, only to find remnants of decaying monuments born of an ancient and mysterious creed. Even for the contemporary viewer, the tree and two wisps of smoke fade into the distance, shrinking reminders of the creation and the near ruin of the Jewish people. It is a scene of missed connections, of sphinx-like spectacles, whose icons evoke a search for meaning that is the very theme of the painting. The panorama is presided over by the visible absence of God, a scenario far from Michelangelo's precise portrayal of the vital moment of creation.

Redefining roles for biblical figures is a major goal of Bak's visual foray into familiar episodes from the Book of Genesis. The narrative of Creation is soon followed by the story of Expulsion from Eden. On the ceiling of the Sistine Chapel Michelangelo combined in one large panel the sequence from Temptation to Expulsion. Bak's versions, two paintings and a drawing, omit the former and concentrate on what he calls "banishment." Thus view-

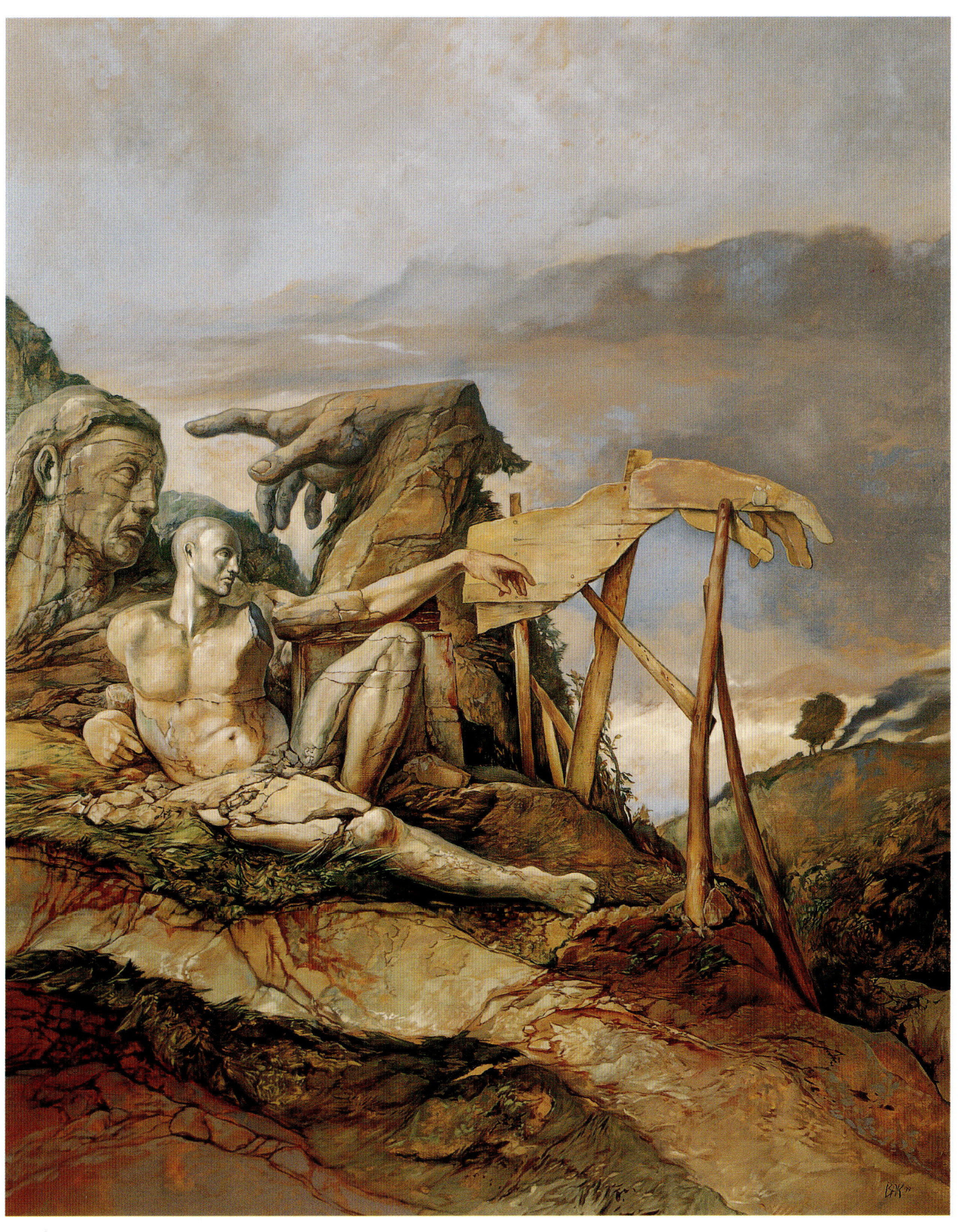

Searching, 1999
Oil on canvas, 40 x 32"

ers have no chance to see the prelapsarian Eve, one of the most beautiful female figures Michelangelo ever painted. In *Banishment* and *Banishment II**, we glimpse a cowering Adam and Eve whose poses are copied from the Sistine source, but whose fear and pain we can attribute to more than the biblical origin in divine displeasure. Michelangelo's pair are driven from a luxuriant Eden by a colorfully-robed angel with a sword; Bak's surrogate angels, with distinctly human features, seem sorrowful themselves. Their metallic wings bind them to earth rather than heaven and their faces are turned away from the supposed objects of God's anger. The background of Michelangelo's panel is open landscape and a boundless sky. Bak's artistic paraphrases offer cramped spaces backed by brick and stone. If we add to this the hand behind the wall in *Banishment* that clasps a rifle, the military shell adjacent to Adam's ossified leg, and the suitcase in the foreground, to say nothing of the floating smoke, we must concede that we are dealing here with a different kind of expulsion, banishment as deportation, a violence that violates the physical integrity of the human couple. In the Book of Genesis Adam and Eve leave Eden to enter time and face their mortality. In Bak they enter history to face their potential annihilation. The cloudlike substance in both paintings vaguely resembles the outline of God in Bak's "creation" episodes, but if punishment for sin has culminated in mass murder, then something has clearly gone awry in the accepted scriptural account of divine intention for the Chosen People.

**page 20 & 21*

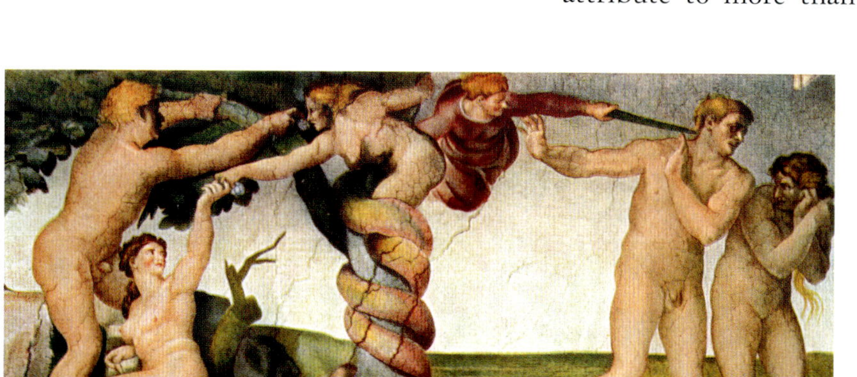

Michelangelo's *Temptation to Expulsion*

Bak takes us back to archetypal moments in that account, inviting us again and again to see them in a different light – through the lens of subsequent darkness. The story of the patriarchs, of Abraham, Isaac, and Jacob, the founding fathers of the people of Israel, and especially of their various contracts with God, are the subject of several paintings in the series, and each one bids us to reinterpret their legendary significance through the experience of contemporary consciousness. Without repudiating their

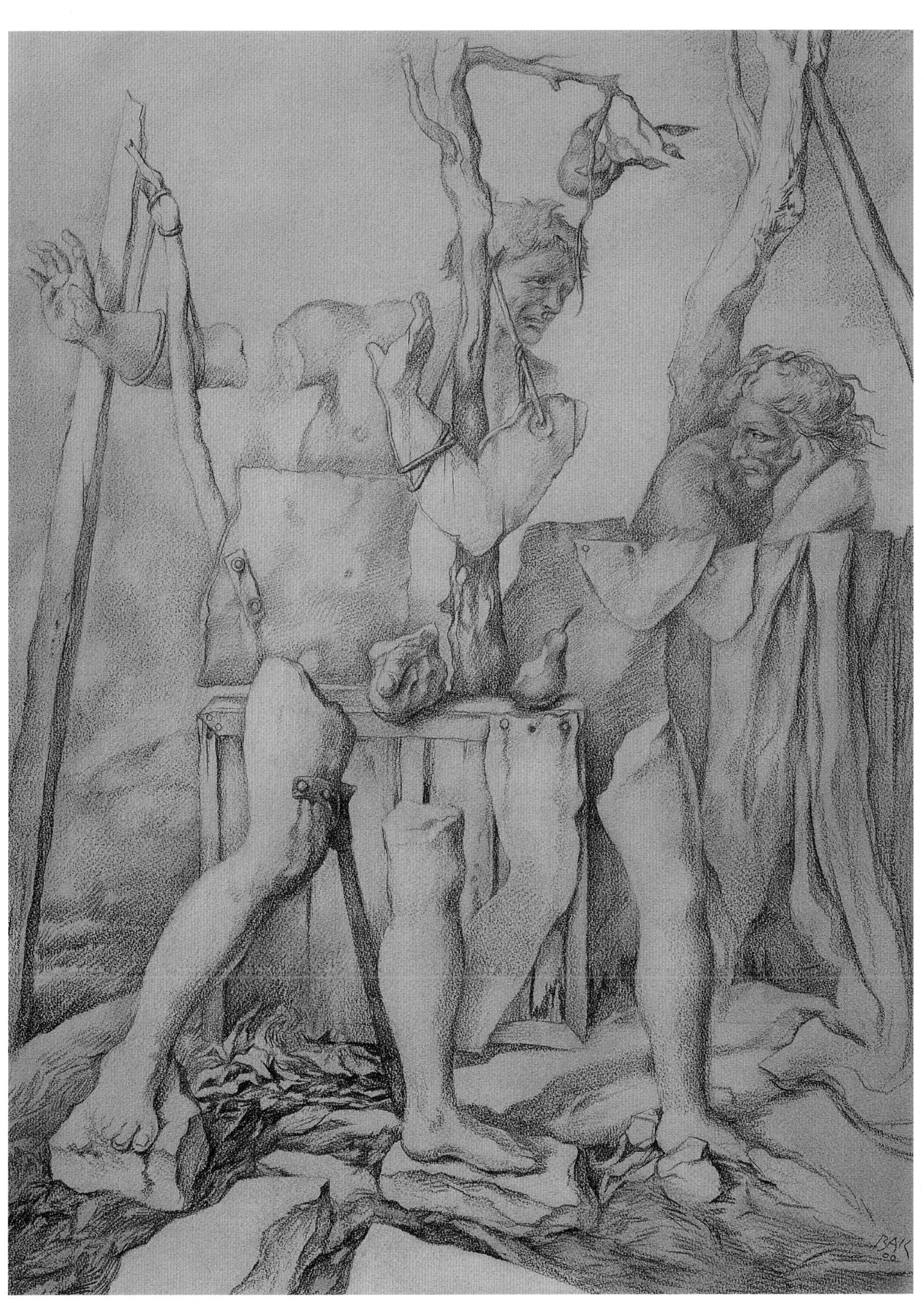

Study for Banishment, 2000
Crayon & pastel on paper,
30 x 22"

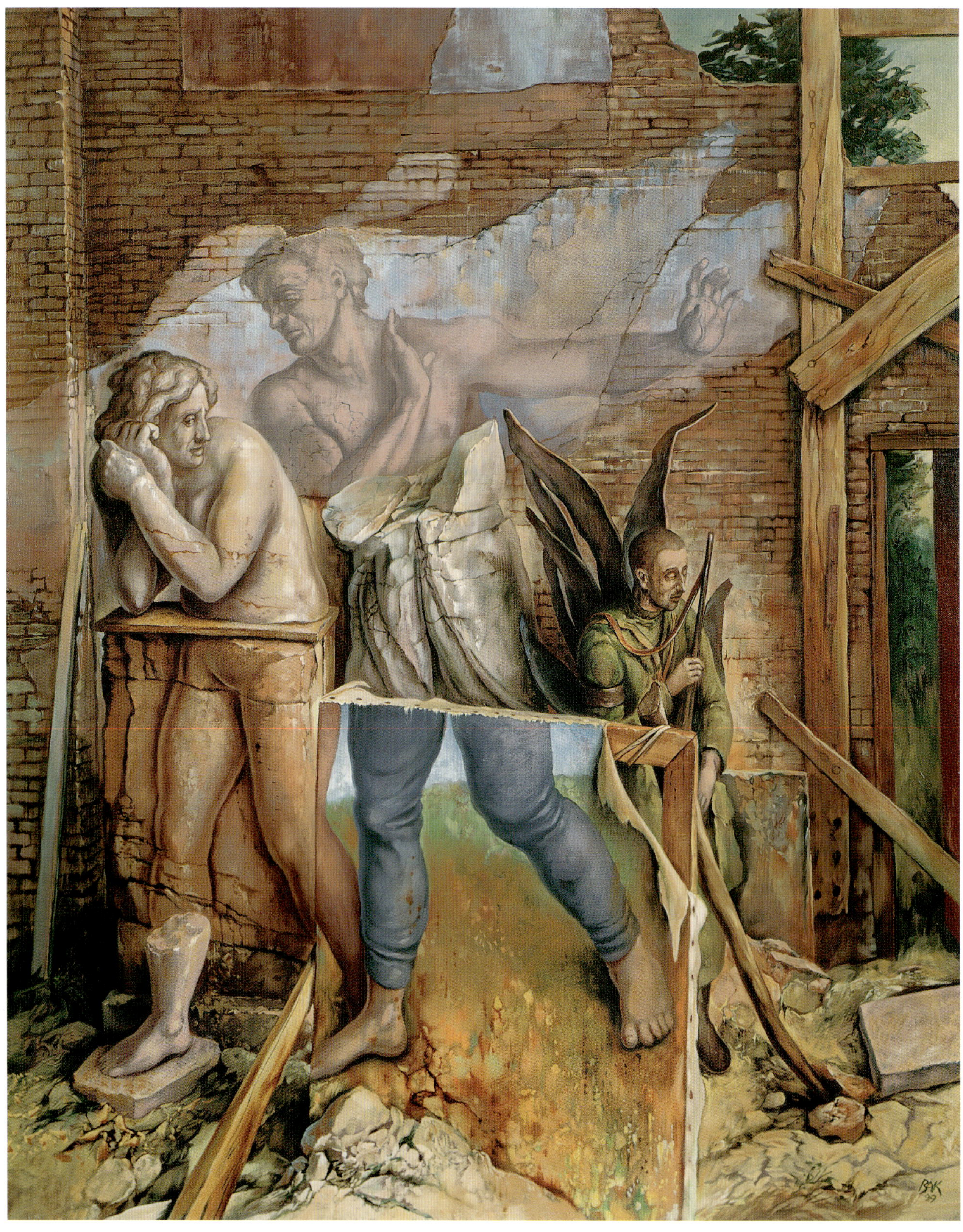

Banishment II, 1999
Oil on canvas, 32 x 26"

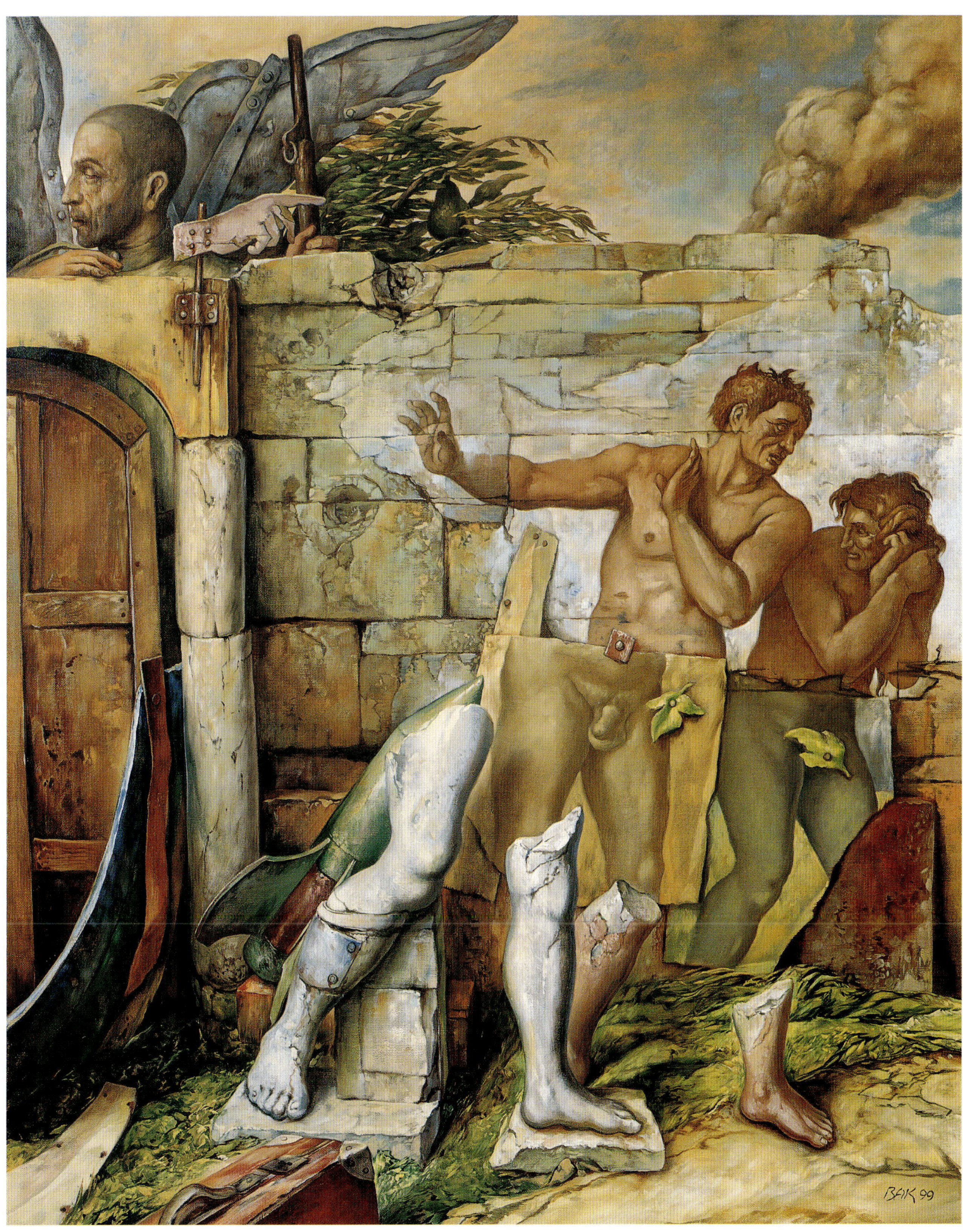

Banishment, 1999
Oil on canvas, 32 x 26"

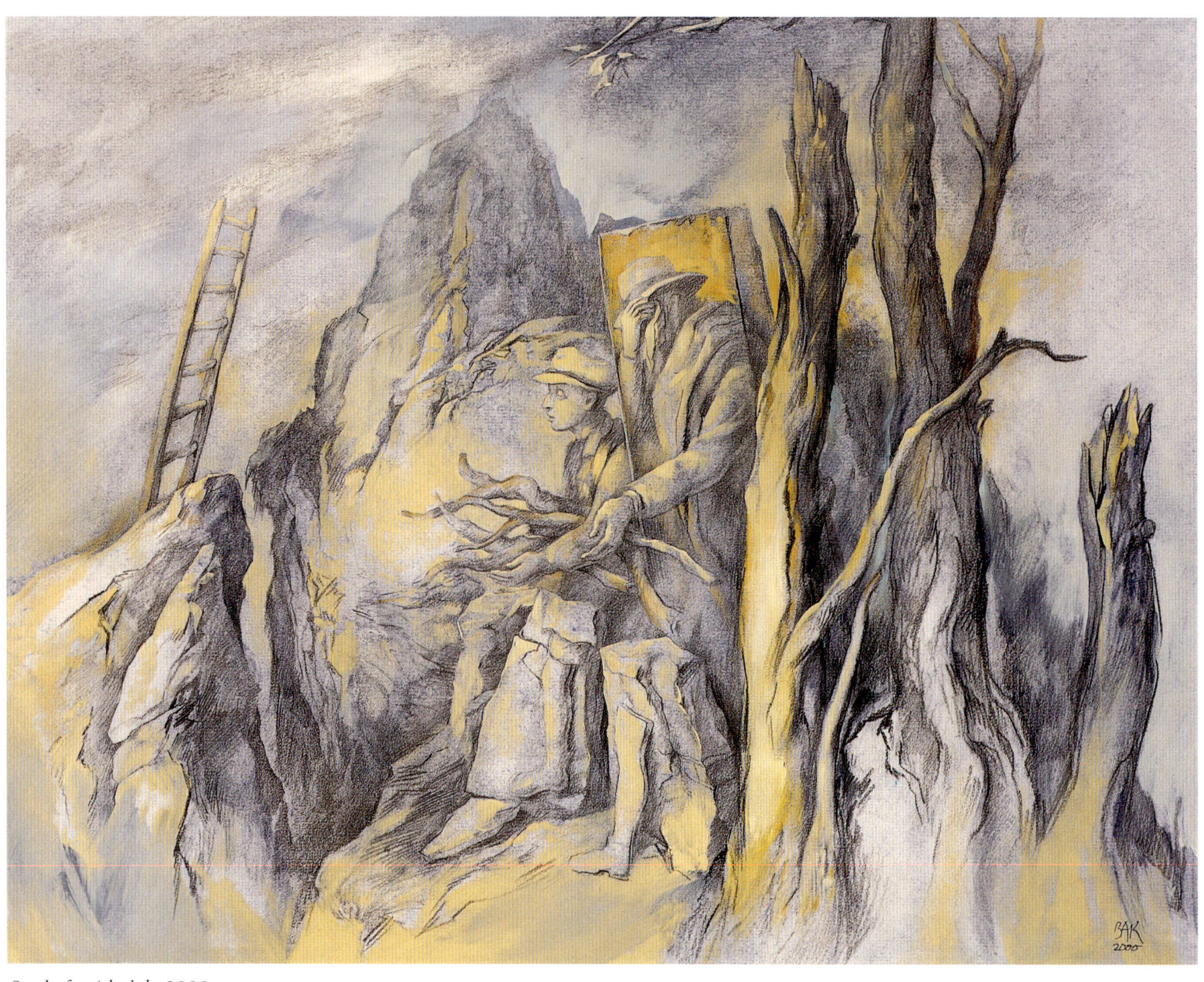

Study for Akedah, 2000
Pencil & oil on paper, 19 x 23 1/2"

importance in the history of the Jewish struggle for identity and the emergence of a unified community, Bak drafts variations on key biblical settings that provoke review of long established religious truths. *Study for Akedah* is set in a desolate mountain landscape with blasted trees. The father and son, the one covering his eyes and the other staring straight ahead, resemble a pair of deportees awaiting their doom more than Abraham prepared to sacrifice his offspring as a sign of unquestioning faith in the hidden purposes of his God. They are encircled by a ghostly yellow haze. The father seems consumed by grief, not driven by obedience, and the washed blue and gray of the sky give no hint of the Deity who has created this test of the ancient patriarch's belief. A ladder rises toward the heavens, but the aura of divinity that endows the Binding of Isaac with its mystery is here notable for its absence from the picture. If the ladder is meant to signify an ascent, its goal is left for the puzzled imagination to uncover. Composed on paper in pencil and oil, the drawing itself suggests an intermediate stage between a specific artistic past and an ambiguous representational future.

*Dress Rehearsal** offers a more finished version of the same theme, but this time rendered with an oriental splendor whose glowing colors resemble the panels on the Sistine Ceiling. Both father and son are blindfolded, cut off from the divine authority that in *Genesis* presided over the scene. Instead, in a sardonic reversal of roles, Abraham himself seems the determined author of the unexplained act of violence, while distressed angels weakly seek to hinder the deed. Their burdensome wings do not identify them as supernatural messengers. They seem prepared to dispute rather than to intervene as heavenly delegates. No ram quivers in a nearby thicket as a surrogate victim. The former agents of God are now like sad-eyed human creatures, Hebrew sages with useless pinions, no rivals to the power of Abraham's mighty scimitar (not the expected knife). In this "dress rehearsal" a holy ritual of sacrifice is metamorphosed into a pagan rite of slaughter. The clash of cultures raises the question of how and why "sacrifice" ceased to be the operative word in the narrative of Jewish suffering, to be replaced by the antiredemptive term "annihilation."

**page 25*

Bak's variation on the Akedah contains a visual mutation on the original story that casts it in a different and unsettling light. No figure in the painting is looking at its most intrusive and disorienting image. Blinded by its blaze of colors and dramatic action, we are in danger of missing it ourselves. Father and son have their eyes shielded, and the angels turn their back to it, as though acknowledging its anomalous presence would further complicate their already difficult task. But one has its wings pinned to the image's surface, the arrow (if we notice it) drawing our eyes away from Abraham's menacing weapon to the even more sinister brick chimney rising beyond the upper margin of the canvas. Was the aborted sacrifice of Isaac only a "dress rehearsal" for the vaster killing of the children of Israel in a later age? How is one to construe the covenant that grew out of Abraham's devotion to God in the unholy light of the subsequent carnage? The disposition of the principal actors in Bak's version, the human confusion that reigns in the absence of divine guidance, the infidel implications of some of the costumes - all conspire to unsettle our view of a scriptural episode that has long troubled commentators because of its pitiless test of a father's divided loyalty. For Bak, the history of the Holocaust has provided fresh reasons for reexamining this ur-text on the role of faith and deliverance in the continuing saga of the Jewish people

A classic example is *Jacob's Dream* (Gen. 28:10-22), to which more than half a dozen paintings from *In a Different Light* are devoted. The biblical story provides a crucial context for Bak's modern variations. On his journey from Beer-sheba, Jacob stops for the night to rest and has a dream:

> and, look, a ramp [usually translated "ladder," though Robert Alter finds this a dubious rendering] was set against the ground with its top reaching the heavens, and, look, messengers of God were going up and coming down it. And, look, the Lord was poised over him and He said, "I, the Lord, am the God of Abraham your father and the God of Isaac. The land on which you lie, to you will I give it and to your seed. And your seed shall be like the dust of the earth and you shall burst forth to the west and the east and the north and the south, and all the clans of the earth shall be blessed through you, and through your seed. And, look, I am with you and I will guard you wherever you go, and I will bring you back to this land, for I will not leave you until I have done that which I have spoken to you."

The repetition of the covenantal promise, especially the vow to "guard you wherever you go" that is made to Jacob and his descendants, may evoke a skeptical response from those who seek continuity between scriptural past and historical present. In contrast to this passage, *In Search of Jacob** presents a visual landscape in disarray, as both the artist and his angels strive in vain to organize incoherent dreamshapes into a pattern of meaning. The shadow ladders have no secure base or any horizon to rise above; they are "landlocked" by the frame of the painting. Three angels, one inverted, bereft of any divine mission, scarcely recognizable as "messengers of

*page 27

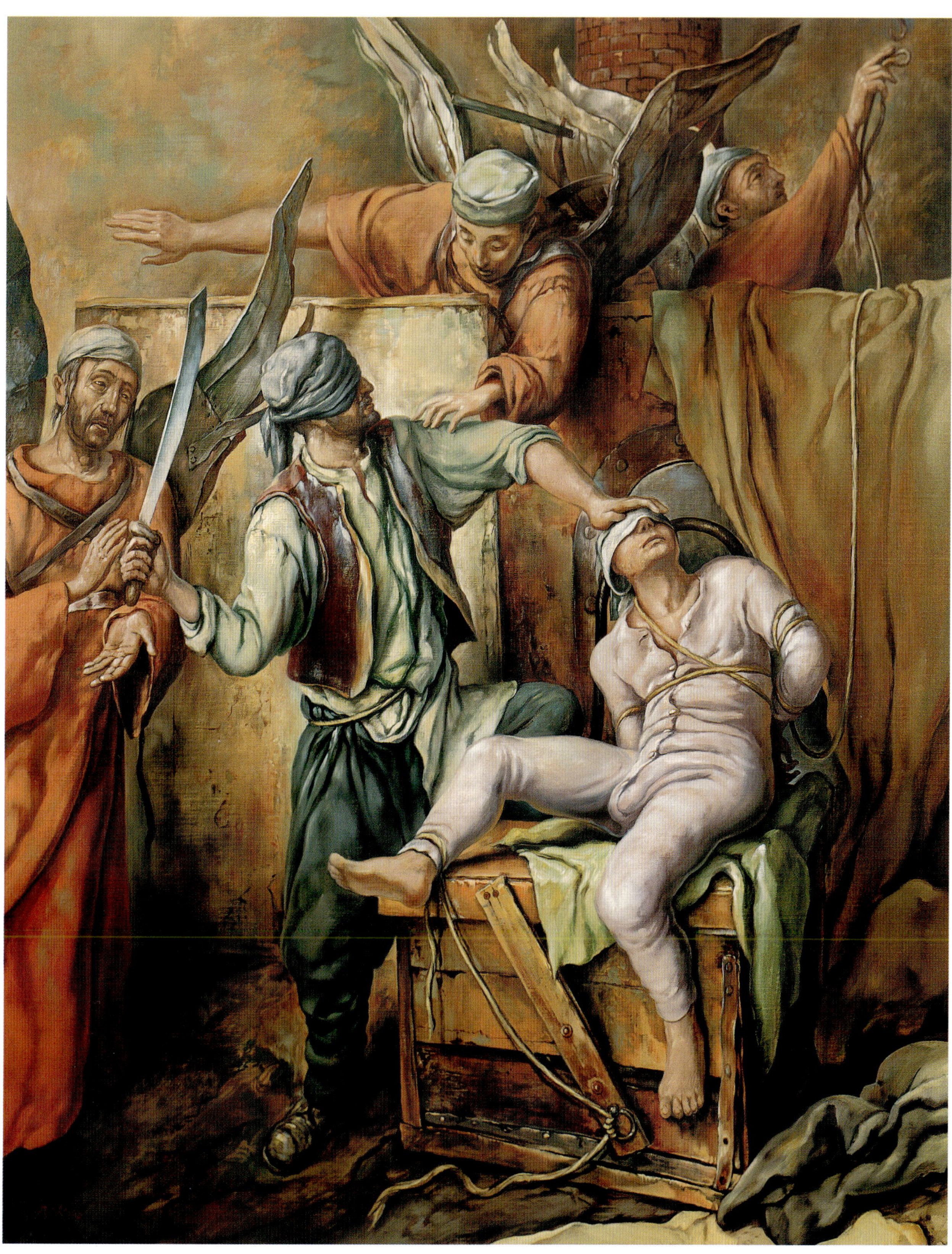

Dress Rehearsal, 1999
Oil on canvas, 40 x 32"

God," stumble upon a sleeping figure (though one might mistake it for a corpse) whom we identify as a fragmented Jacob. Whatever epiphany *Genesis* intended, here the revelation is reserved for the viewer, not the dreamer; a glowing robe drapes the lower half of the sleeper, but adjacent to this once sanctified but now bloodied garment lies the striped apparel of the concentration camp inmate. This ominous scrap of cloth forces the post-Holocaust mind to view God's promise to Jacob that "your seed shall be like the dust of the earth" with a certain ironic dismay. The biblical Jacob's reply to God's pledge of protection intensifies the irony of the merged images: he consecrates a pillar of stone at the site of the dream and names it Bethel, the House of God. But the canny Jacob makes this a *provisional* offering: "If the Lord God be with me and guard me on this way...then the Lord will be my God." When Jacob's column of homage became the Holocaust chimney of death, Bak and his audience were left to meditate on the significance of Jacob's conditional bargain. If the covenant were a two-sided pact from the beginning, how reliable was the divine assurance that: "I will not leave you until I have done that which I have spoken to you?"

But if time has undermined the security of the Jews, it has also altered the roles of the angels who once brought spiritual inspiration to mankind from the Master of the universe. The figure in

**page 28*

*Rainbow Angel** inhabits a landscape of ruin, confined rather than liberated by fragments of ladders with broken rungs. Her split visage reflects the uncertainties of her divided mission: is she here to bring assurance from God, or to mourn with man? Her multiple hands confirm the complexity of her task, as they seem to alternate between gestures of blessing and appeal. Encumbered by metallic wings, encased in stone, seated beside the remains of the omnipresent crematorium chimney, she exudes little of her spiritual origins. Several biblical scholars have noted that stones are Jacob's personal motif; the same might be said of the artist Samuel Bak, though in this portrait of a handicapped angel (as well as in numerous other of his paintings) they form a cultic marker of a different sort.

The Book of Genesis is a textual representation of the birth of monotheism, of a contract between the human and the divine that still comprises the basis for Jewish belief. Bak's personal experience of the Holocaust, as well as the fate of European Jewry

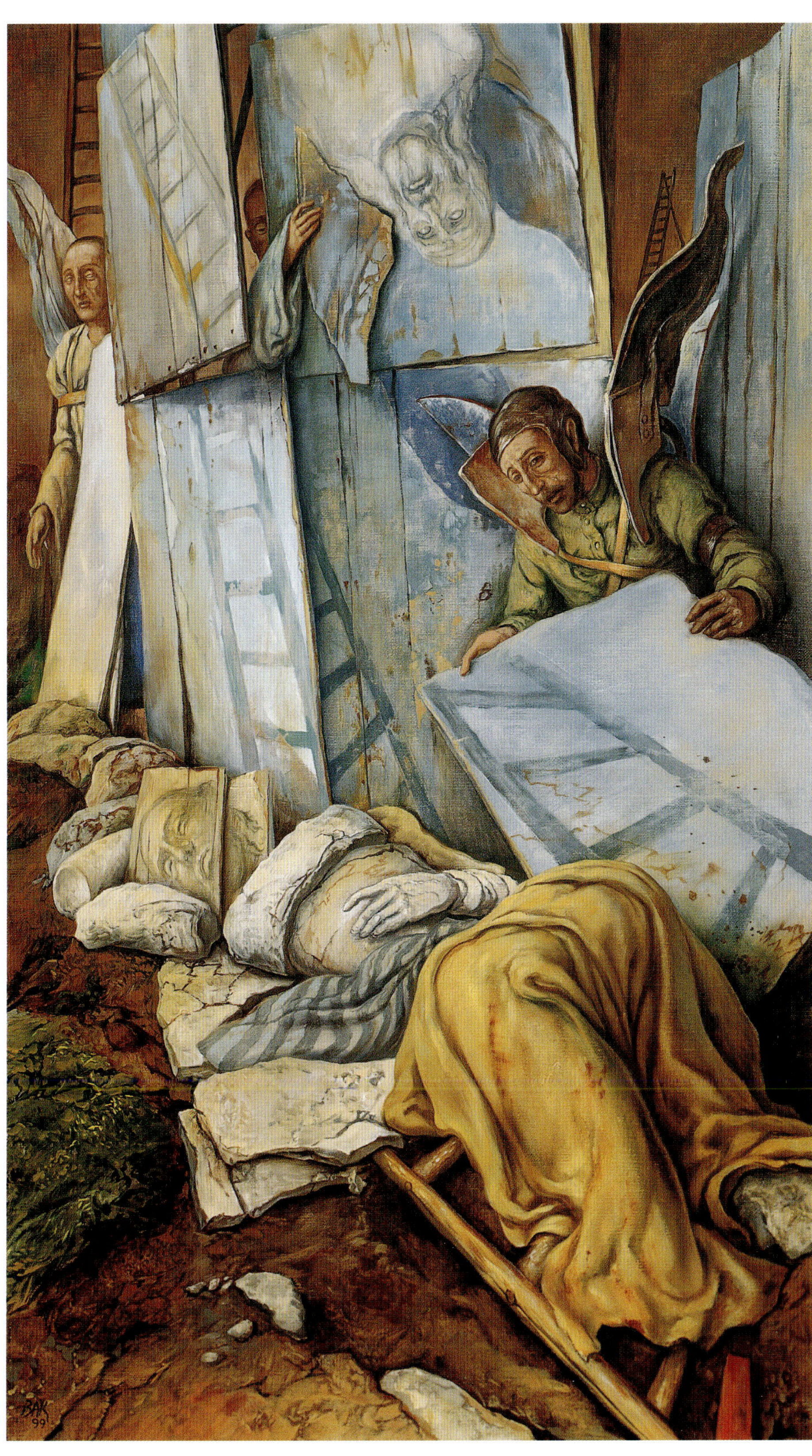

In Search of Jacob, 1999
Oil on canvas, 32 x 18"

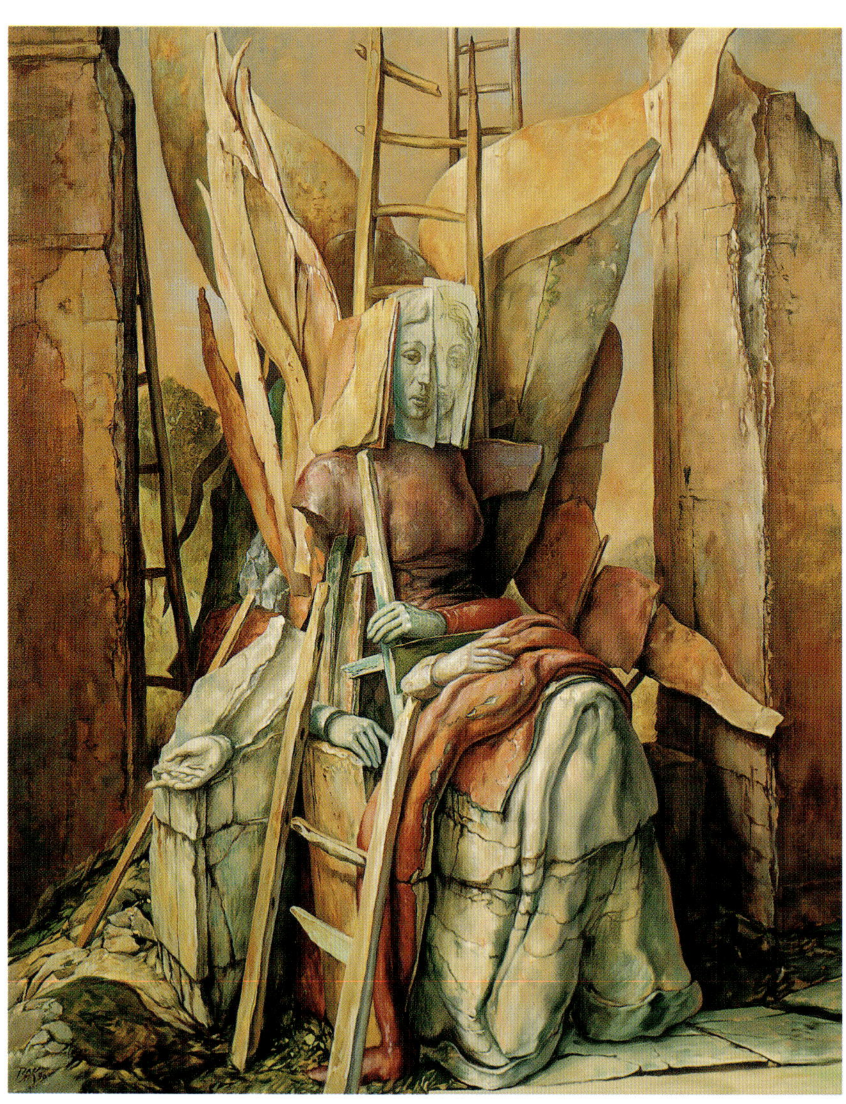

Rainbow Angel, 1999
Oil on canvas, 32 x 26"

during that period, casts doubt on the stability of that contract. His vision fluctuates between the disorder of *Looking for the Dreamer*, where angels themselves seem victims of a universe caught in the throes of chaos, and *About Dreaming**, whose images simultaneously rouse memories of ruin and the need to reestablish meaning in a time of loss. Here the empty shoes echo the ghost of the murdered boy of *Self Portrait* (from Landscapes of Jewish Experience); the column of smoke rising behind the head of the sightless angel keeps the dreamer from sleep as he searches for a textual explanation of the pilgrimage toward death that his own interrupted journey could not have foreseen. The facing hands that once signaled the creation of Adam now point toward Jacob's brow and the volume he

**page 30*

is reading, as if to warn us that any meaning to be reclaimed from the ongoing narrative of Jewish destiny must be sought in the mind and the lore of man. A member of the "people of the book," Jacob looks downward toward the written page, apparently oblivious to the angelic presence blocked from his vicinity by an intervening wall. Is he searching for divine assurance, or a human truth? Is the upward-pointing finger on the right a prop left over from an earli-

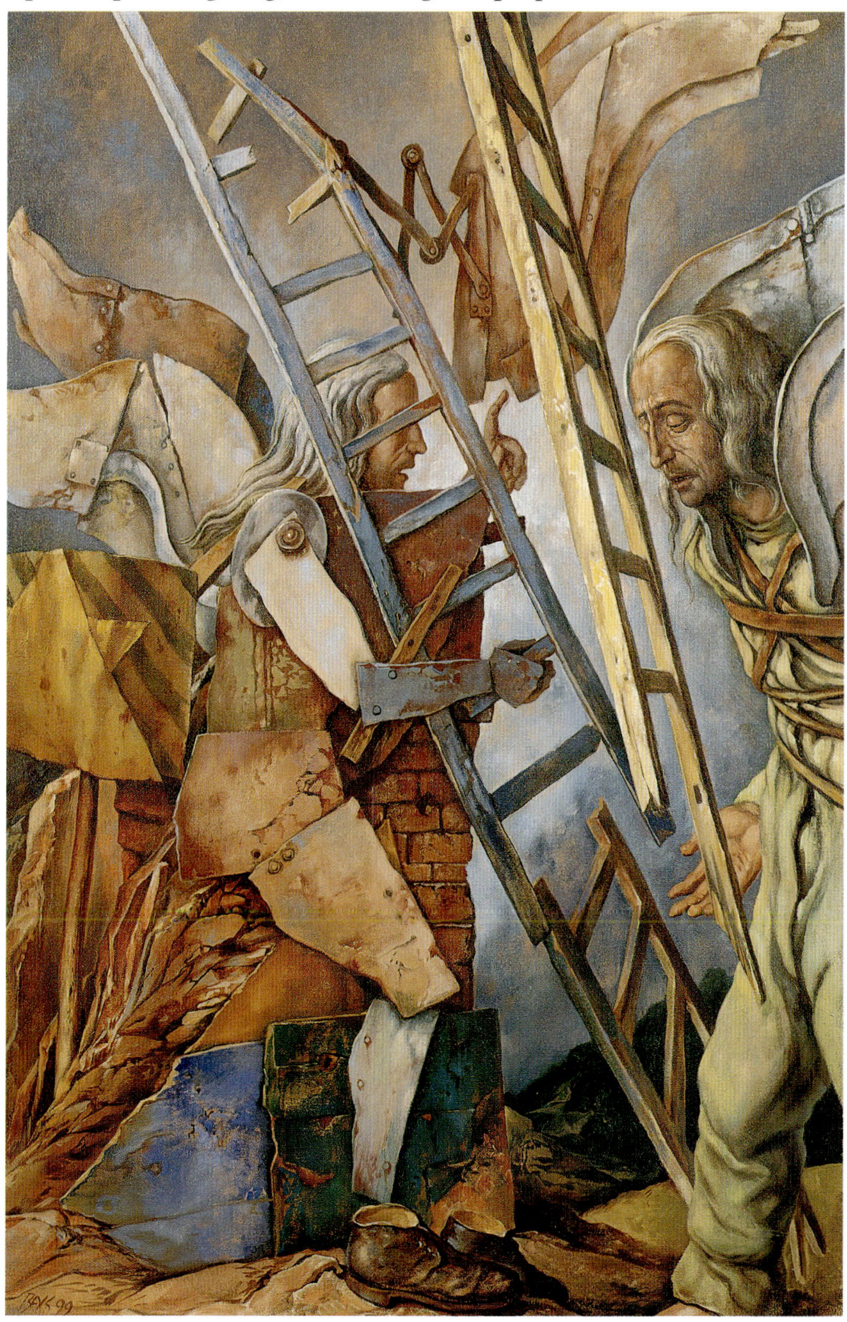

Looking for the Dreamer, 1999
Oil on canvas, 30 x 20"

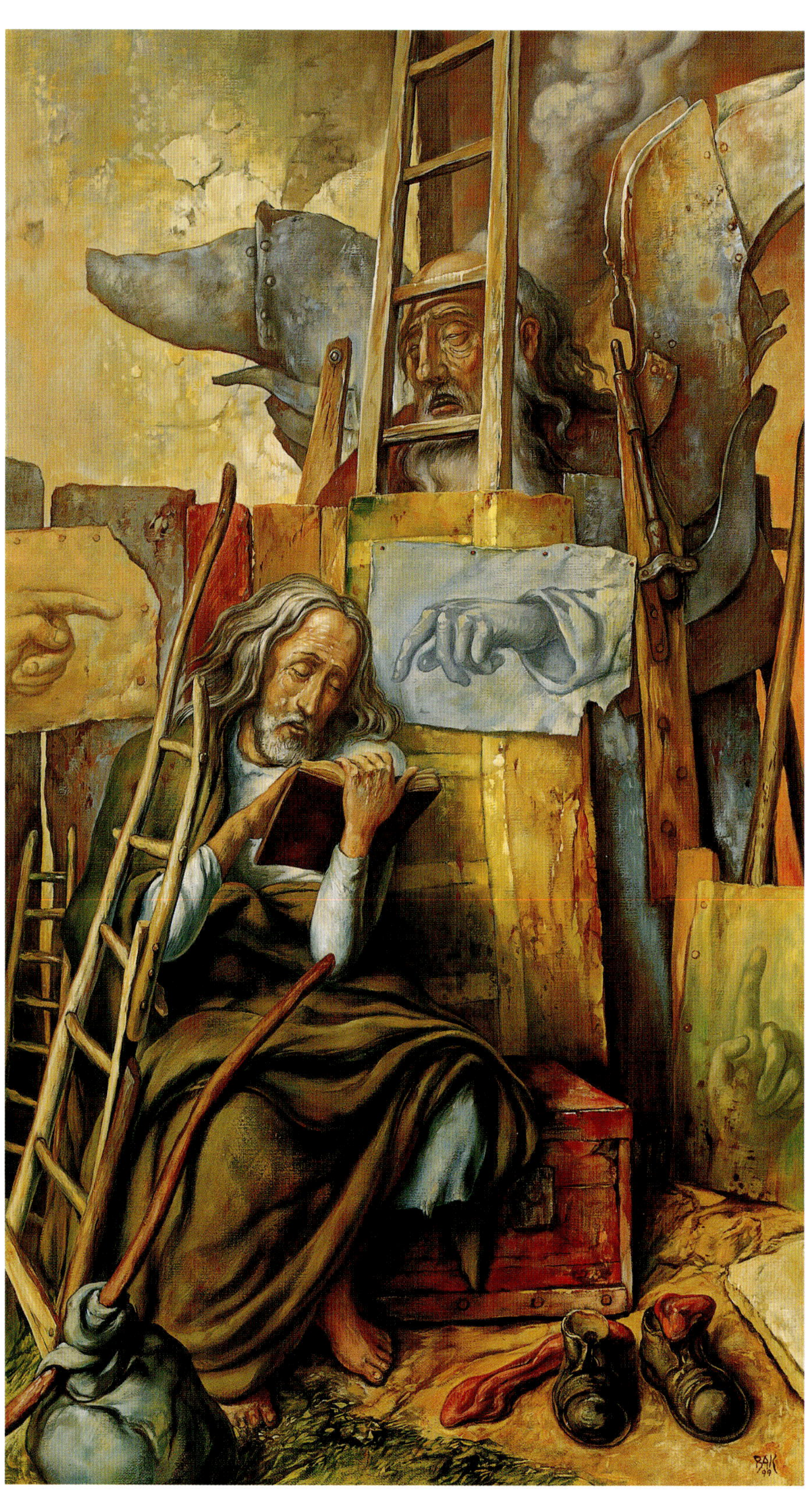

About Dreaming, 1999
Oil on canvas, 32 x 18"

er performance or a legitimate option that the "actors" in the painting ignore, leaving the spectator with the choice of investigating the direction it proposes?

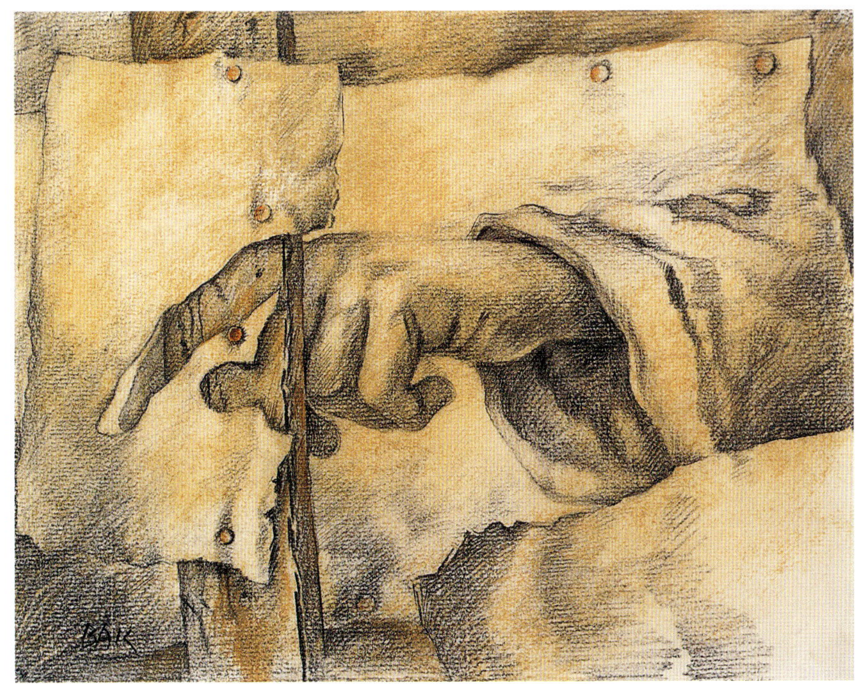

Study for "About Dreaming", 1999
Crayons & pastel on paper, 9 1/2 x 12 1/2"

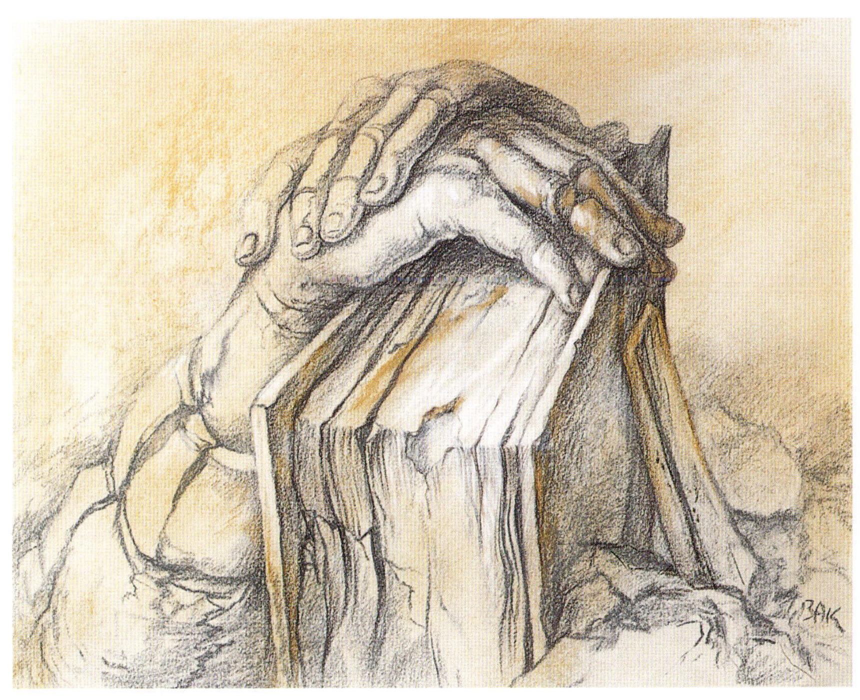

Study After Durer, 1999
Crayons & pastel on paper, 9 1/2 x 12 1/2"

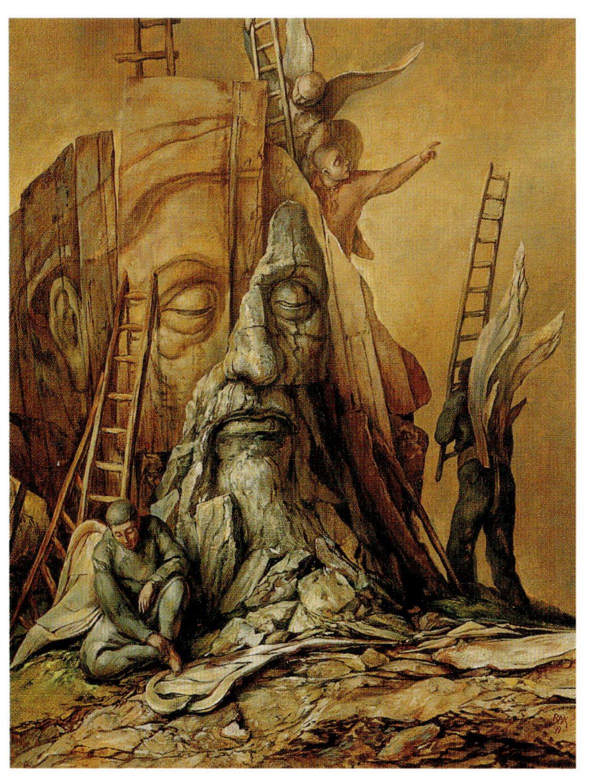

Study for the Dreaming Jacob, 1999
Oil on canvas, 18 x 14"

When history recedes, men consider building monuments to a past that would otherwise disappear. As time erodes memory, myths accrue around what was once an actual reality, until finally its origins remain shrouded in mystery. In *Study for the Dreaming Jacob* and *Dreaming Jacob*, Bak reverses this tendency as some of his angels shed their wings and become servants to an earthly task. Representation has replaced inspiration as their daily labor, as if in their curtailed mission they now served not God but the needs of art. Their ladders are no longer avenues to heaven but mere scaffolding for the construction of a Jewish sphinx whose patriarchal aspect will be unmistakable to future generations. The dreaming Jacob is the author of his own appearance, a potential creator whose personal vision emerges from a human impulse to endure. The angelic helpers now seem committed to a secular end – noble, but no longer rooted in scriptural authority.

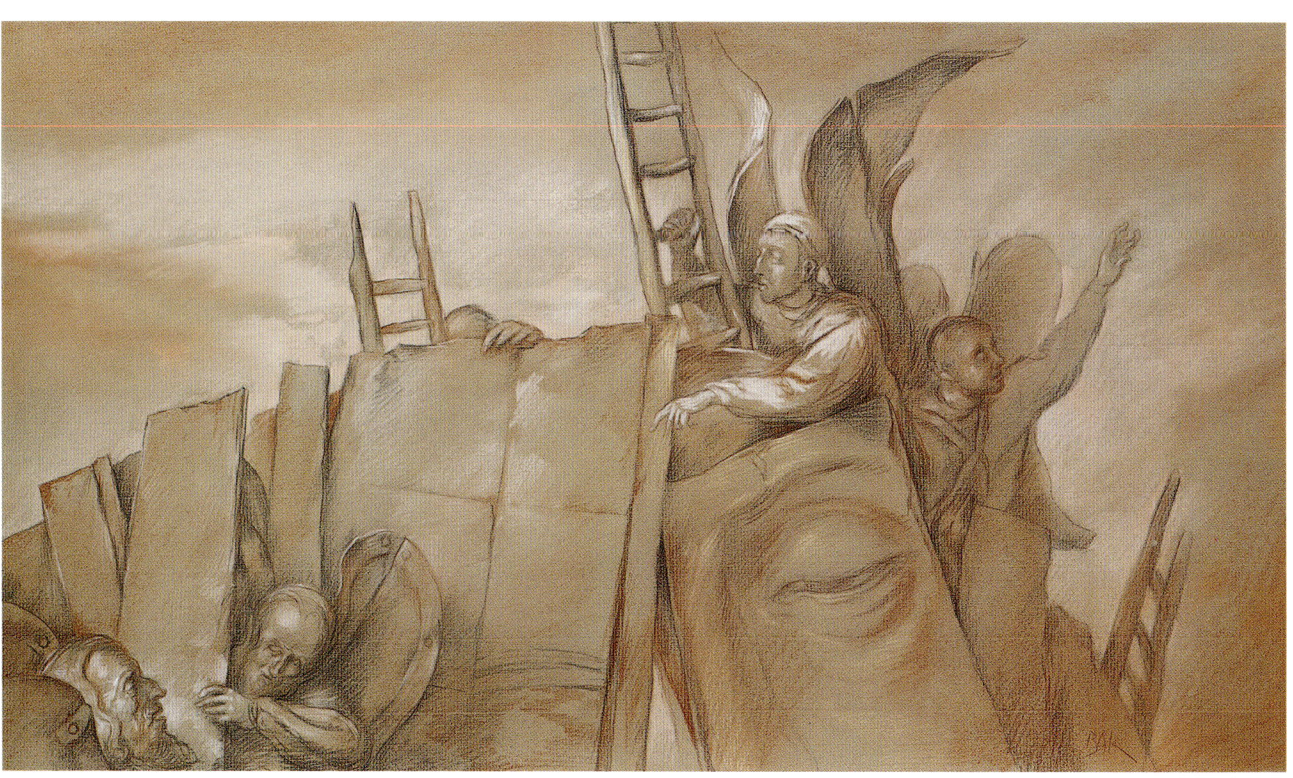

Study for the Dreaming Jacob, 1999
Pastel on paper, 11 x 19"

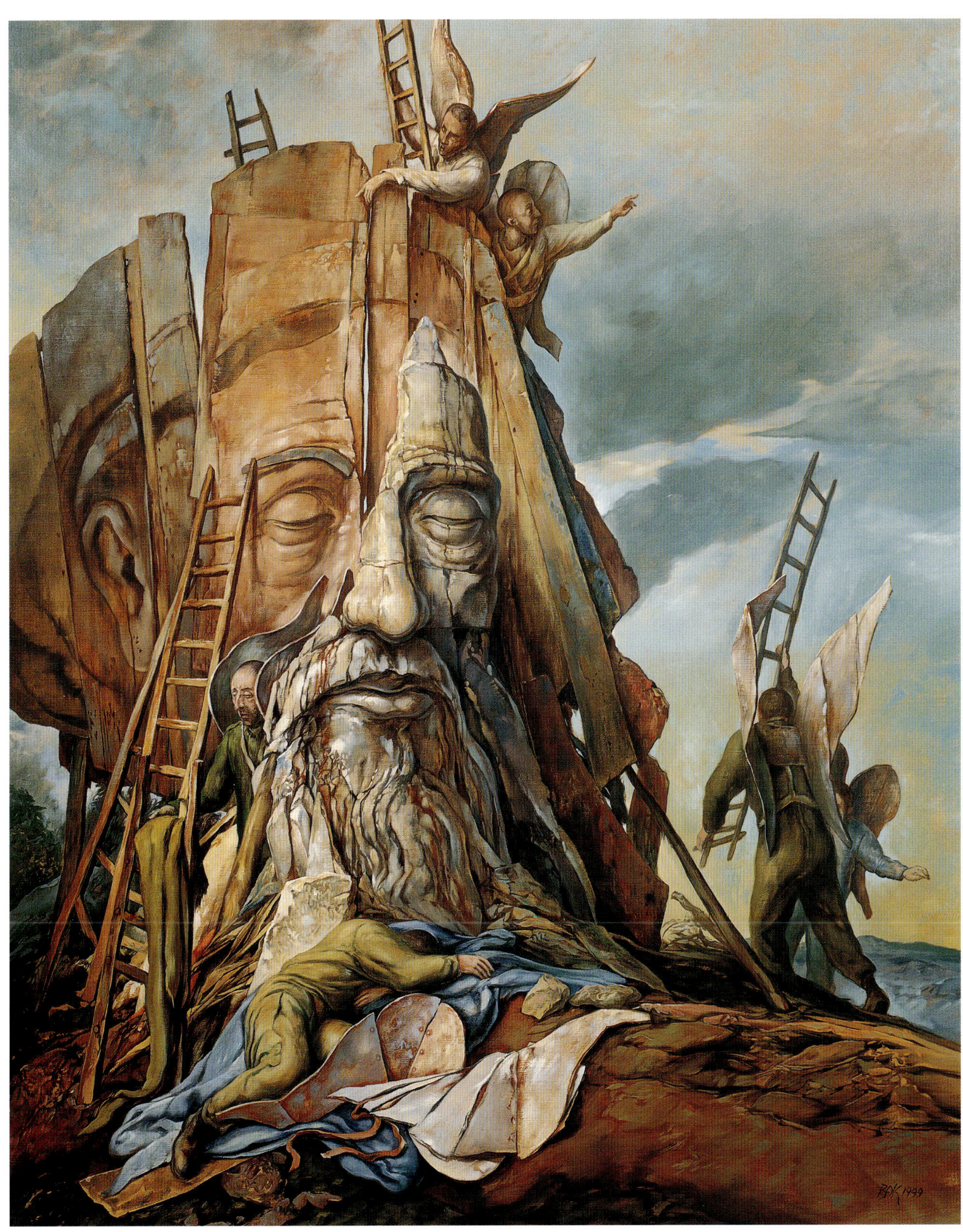

Dreaming Jacob, 1999
Oil on canvas, 40 x 32"

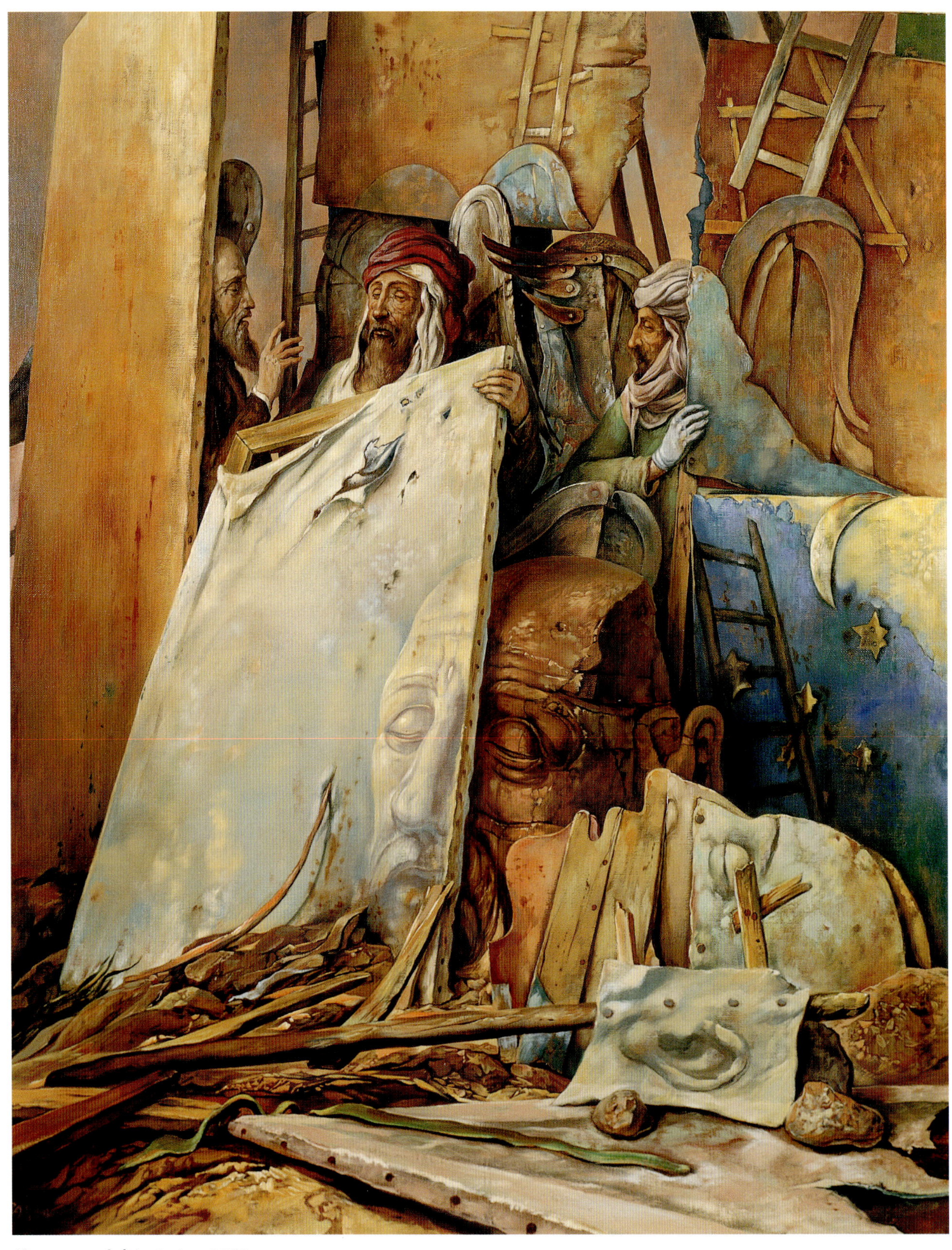

Dreamers and their Artists, 1999
Oil on canvas, 32 x 26"

This current of thought seems confirmed by both setting and title of *Dreamers and their Artists*, where the theme of Creation is transmuted into the site for a different kind of invention, an artist's studio. Angels garbed in exotic array support unfinished canvases, perhaps debating how to rescue from the debacle of time abiding portraits of their flawed spiritual heritage. The clutter in the background obscures the heavens, while one painting reveals a vivid blue sky with floating golden Stars of David alongside a dim ladder that in the biblical text had a clear symbolic meaning. The dream was once an epiphany, a form of divine revelation. But as the dreamer now lies, once more corpse-like, amidst the debris of history, the artist is left with the responsibility of animating his inert form and transferring it into a visual record that will transcend mortal and monumental decay. In this way art supplies the ravages of history with a lasting habitation, offering them up for scrutiny and analysis to future generations. The act of restoration in the studio becomes a bold alternative to the prior parallel practice of spiritual repair.

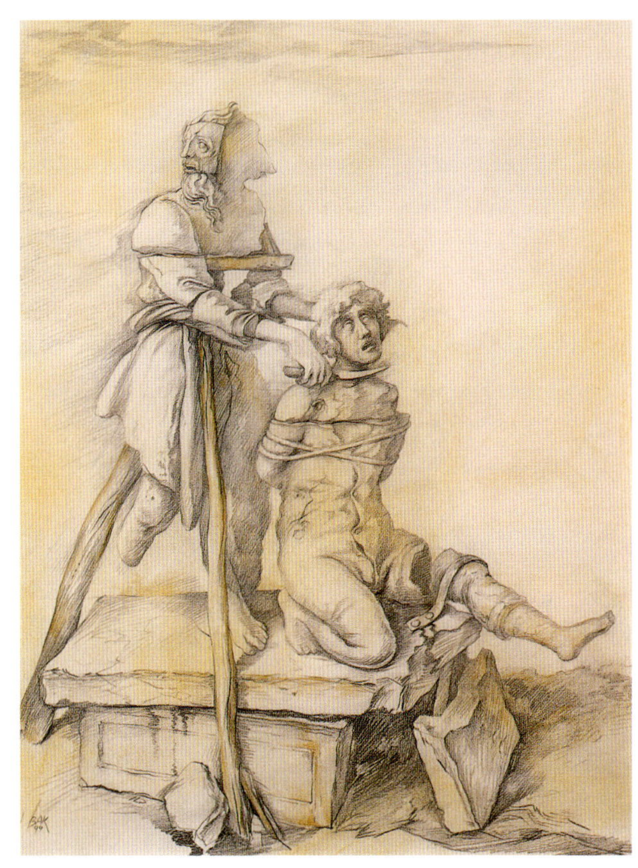

After Mantegna, 1999
Pencil & pastel on paper, 23 3/4 x 19"

We will return to the notion of "repair" later, since it constitutes an important theme of *In a Different Light*. Here we need only note that for Bak it bears the implication of mending rather than total renewal. The challenge is dramatically portrayed by *Isaac's Dream**, on whose crowded terrain past and present coalesce amidst a salvo of multilayered imagery. The eye rises vertically through the composition, from the foreground site of the rejected sacrifice to the background stone ship belching heavenward smoke from its cremated victims, a modern vessel of death that has replaced Noah's ark of life. Abraham is represented as the familiar aged Jew and Isaac appears peering over a wooden barricade with the face of the boy artist from *Self Portrait*,[1] who in turn is associated with the doomed child from the Warsaw ghetto. Isaac's right hand is extended in a gesture of appeal, encircled not by a binding rope but by phylacteries of prayer. Appeal to whom? On the wooden barrier behind which the father protects his son appear two *yods,*

**page 36*

1. Langer, Lawrence, Landscapes of Jewish Experience. University Press of New England, Hanover and Pucker Art Publications, 1997, Boston, p. 37.

one of the Hebrew designations of God's name, but the only "response" Isaac receives is locked in the mystery of the letters painted on large wooden panels that hang from ropes reaching beyond the upper border of the picture, as if dangled by the hands of some taunting divine puppeteer. They spell *malakh*, which means angel, but the secular inference of the spirit become word should not be lost on the viewer. Isaac's dream is not a nocturnal vision, nor has it any scriptural authority. If he is not thinking of his own escaped fate, can he be imagining the doom of his seed generations in the future? And of how, as a mature artist, he will use his beseeching hand to depict the voyage from holiness to horror, from the place of covenant to the place of suffocation, and how through his art he will try to reconcile that holiness with this horror?

But Isaac's waking dream includes more. The inverted rainbow in the left foreground is another item of spiritual disrepair that must be included in any integrative vision of a mended present. It is a token of God's promise to Noah never again to destroy His creatures by flood. But in Genesis it was also a reaffirmation: "This is the sign of the covenant I have established between Me and all the flesh that is on the earth." [Gen. 9: 17-18] As our glance moves from the discarded rainbow past the leaning ladders of Jacob's dream that no longer form an avenue to heaven, then traces the space separating the altar of stone from the columns of mass dying, memories of the Jewish journey from the sacrificial test of faith to the unredeemed and unredeemable Holocaust hover over the scene. No wonder the eyes of Abraham and Isaac in this painting are saddened by the prospect before them. The mind must first comprehend the desolate inference of this voyage before it can be transferred to canvas. The twisted roots of the dying trees – once perhaps trees of life and moral knowledge – are searching for new nourishment as both viewer and artist confront the dilemma of restoring order to the shambles of this spiritual landscape.

Isaac's Dream, 1999
Oil on canvas, 40 x 50"

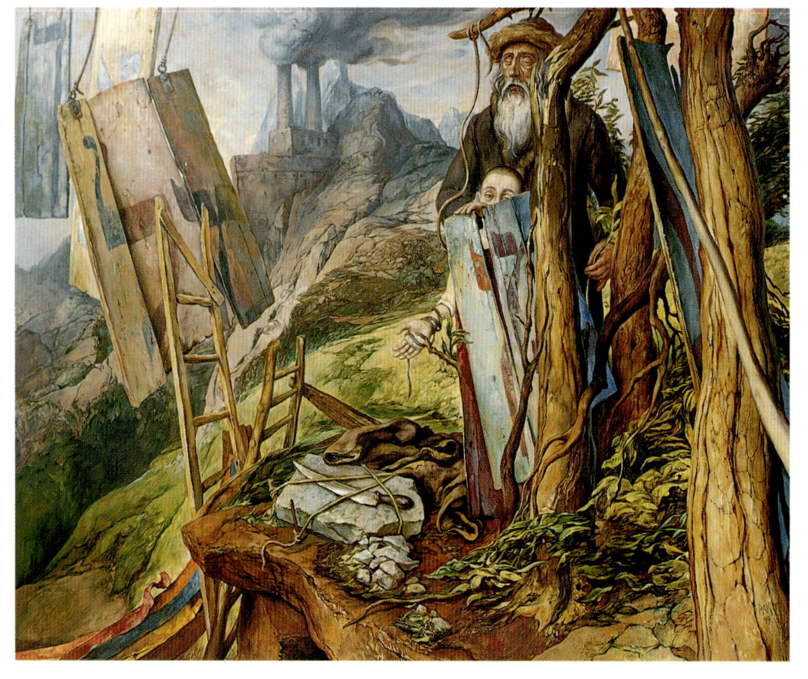

Isaac's Dream,
(detail)

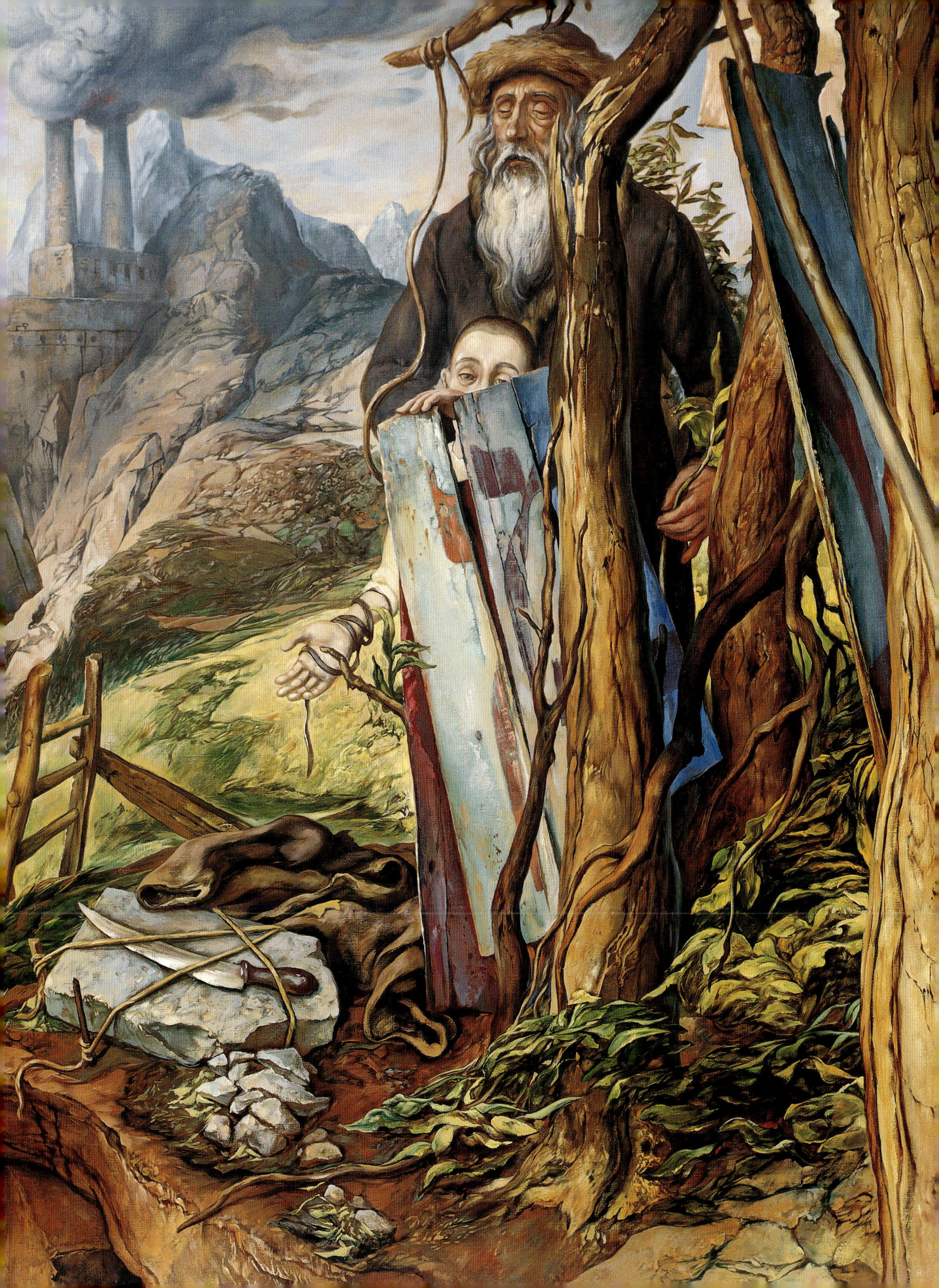

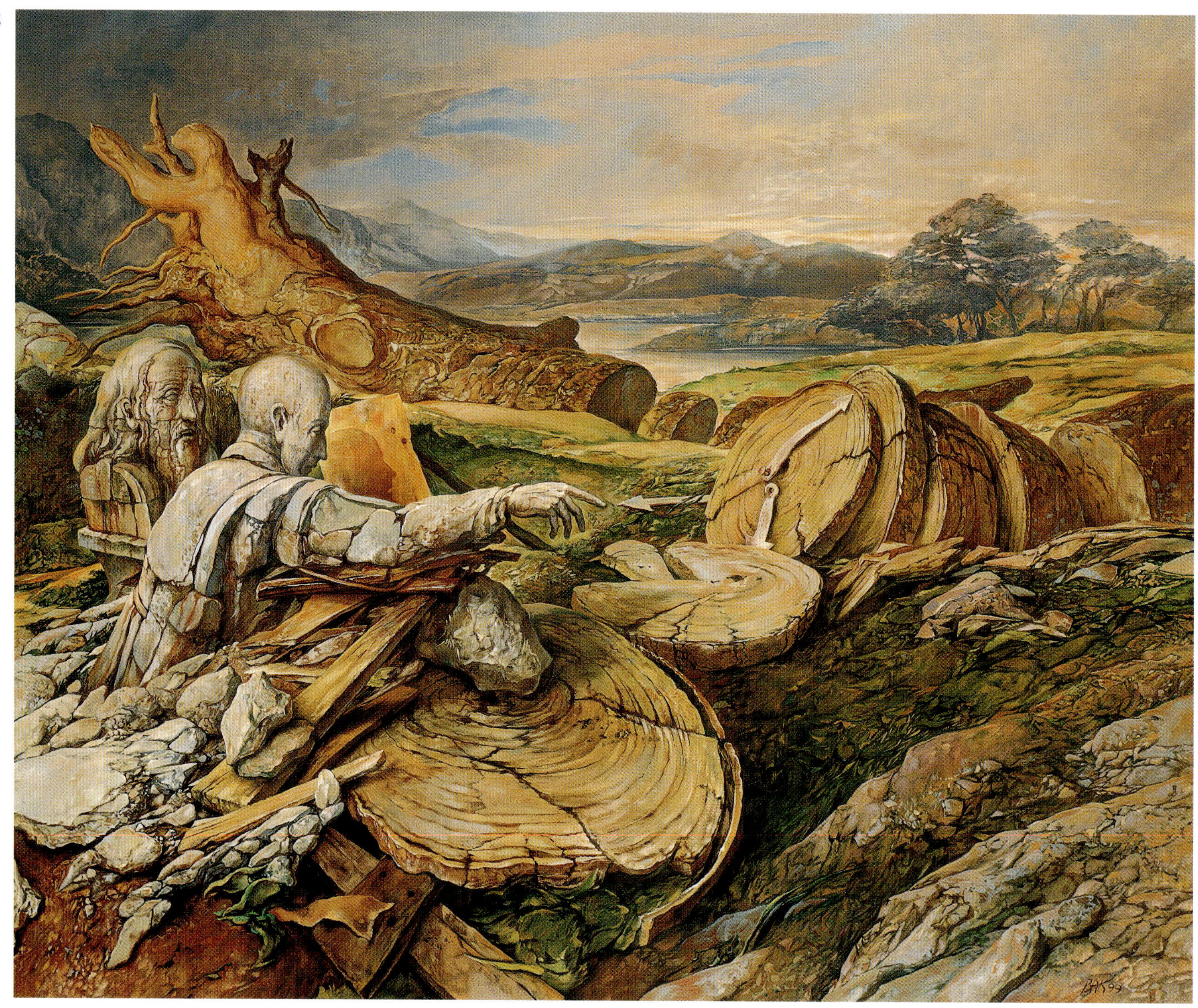

Timepiece, 1999
Oil on canvas, 32 x 40"

Where Time Used to Flow, 1999
Oil on canvas, 16 x 30"

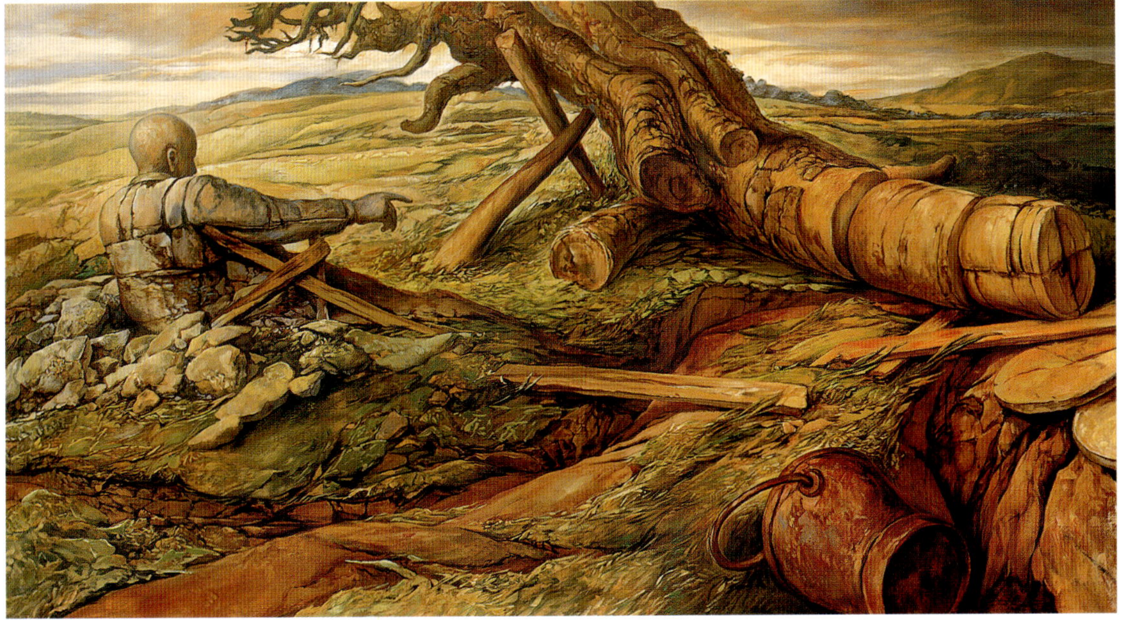

Robert Alter observes that: "the literary prose of the Bible turns everywhere on significant repetition, not variation." Visual equivalents of this stylistic idea abound – Monet's numerous Water Lilies come instantly to mind. They may be seen as artistic reactions to the biblical admonition to be fruitful and multiply, duplicating the initial act of Creation through the renewal of forms. If they resemble each other, as they do in the example of Monet, they signify no lack of invention but are rather forceful reminders that a view reveals more of its beauty through subtle shifts in perspective. Since surfaces, colors, and the play of light varied on the single

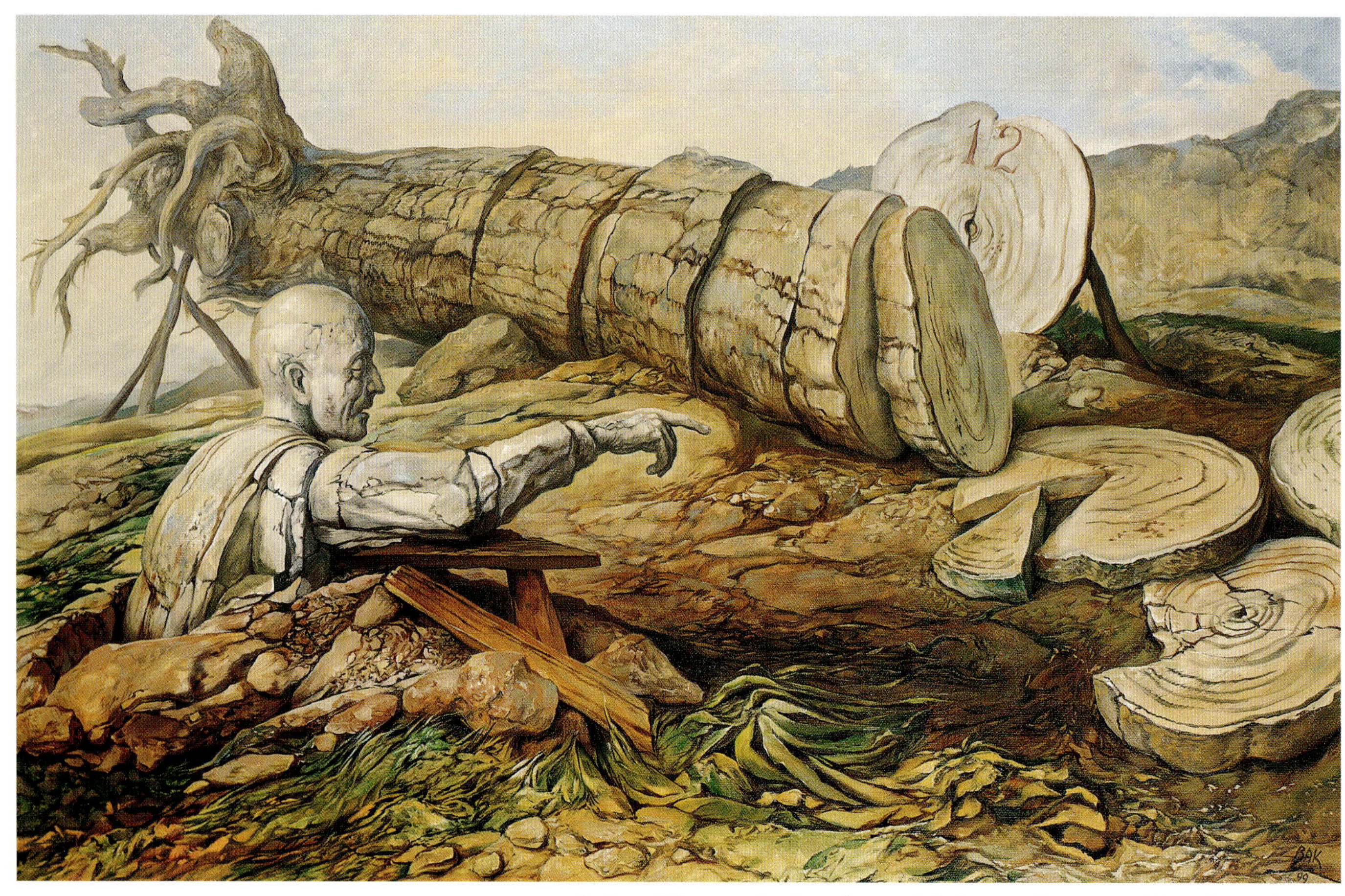

Creation of Time, 1999
Oil on canvas, 20 x 30"

pond that Monet depicted, multiple versions could only enhance the attraction of his subjects – that is, when they were seen "in a different light." When Samuel Bak addresses the more painful theme of time in a half dozen paintings from his cycle, the landscapes are similar though not identical. Each contains a version of a tree, newly uprooted, or as a dead trunk, intact or sliced and dissected – all reminiscent of that tree and its fruit "whose mortal taste," as Milton wrote, "brought death into the world, and all our woe/and loss of Eden." Bak imitates the original creative moment in a re-creation that appears to substitute a statuary Adam for God to rectify an omission from the primordial design. When God created day and night, He meant them to exist within a context of eternity. In *Creation of Time* Bak introduces a complex paradox for our contemplation: insofar as the human creature is a victim of mortality, time conquers man, but as the artist renders a permanent portrayal of that dilemma, art conquers time. The clock face made from a slab of tree rings may be Bak's reminder that the best way to rectify the absence of infinity is to understand time and use it wisely. But the stone Adam's pointing finger recalls another legacy, the missing figure of Michelangelo's mighty anthropomorphic God. The aging tree rings seem a humble substitute for that absent presence.

This thought might well lead to the visual confrontation in *Debate*, where stunted tree limbs reach out to welcome Adam's now habitual gesture. Remembering the solidly sculptured substance of Michelangelo's Adam and God, we are struck by the diminished human status of Bak's creatures. Adam is a crude assemblage of brick and stone, while his aged companion wears a ghastly mask attached to fragments of wood. One hand is detached from his body; it rests on a book held sideways, as if in vain attempt to learn whether an ancient (scriptural?) text can provide guidance to the dubious scene before him. Nature and man seek alliance in a deserted landscape, while a severed forearm lies forlornly in the exact center of the picture. Perhaps the "debate" of the title concerns how to restore a living movement of brotherly amity to its inert hand. When a human face finally intrudes in

Debate, 1999
Oil on canvas, 16 x 30"

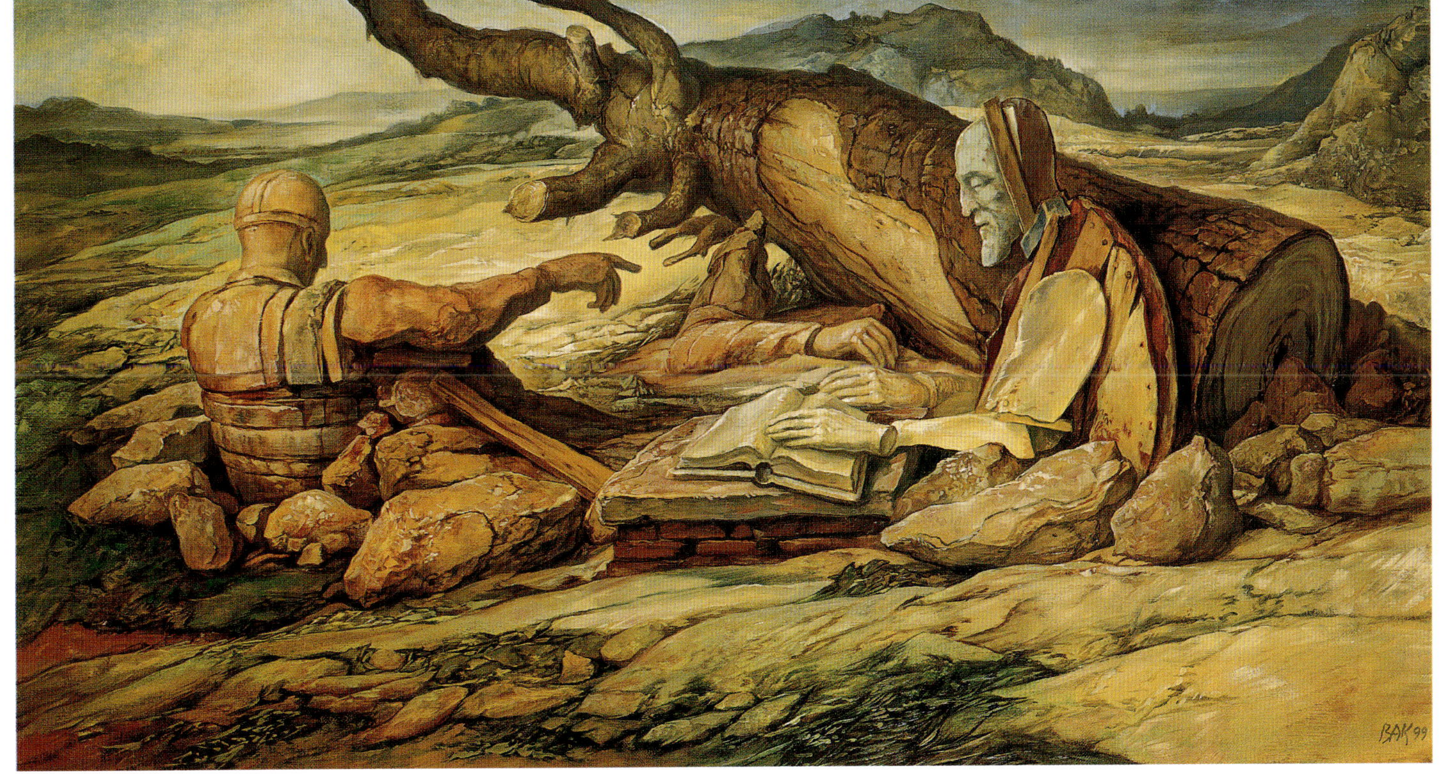

At the Root of Things and a human hand of authentic flesh appears as an extension of its physical self painted on canvas, we get a vivid clue to how art can stay the decay of time. Since the outstretched arms of the figures in this painting cannot stop the uprooted tree from tumbling into the abyss, some other form of representation must get to "the root of things."

But if the main question is the preservation of roots, one is compelled to ask which roots form the principal source of the Jewish chronology. In *About Time* the effigy of Adam, or his descendant in the guise of Everyman, receives silent counsel from two faces amidst a landscape suffused with hues of blood and fire. It is easily the most sinister painting in the "time" group. The tree is a fallen, segmented column of wood, surmounted by an intact column of stone which summons us to a phase of Jewish destiny that time has wrought beyond the frontiers of biblical narrative. Adam

At the Root of Things, 1999
Oil on canvas, 20 x 30"

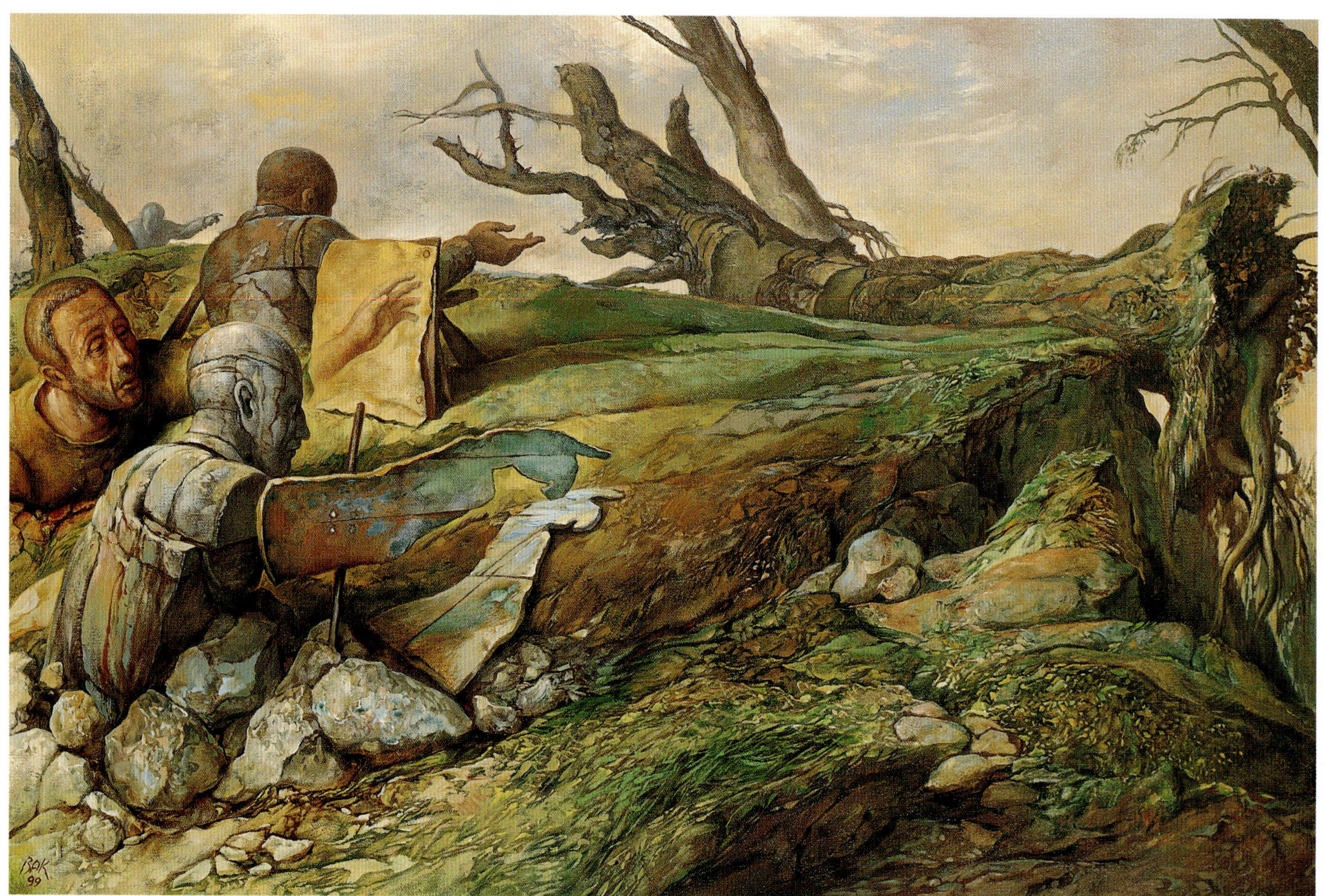

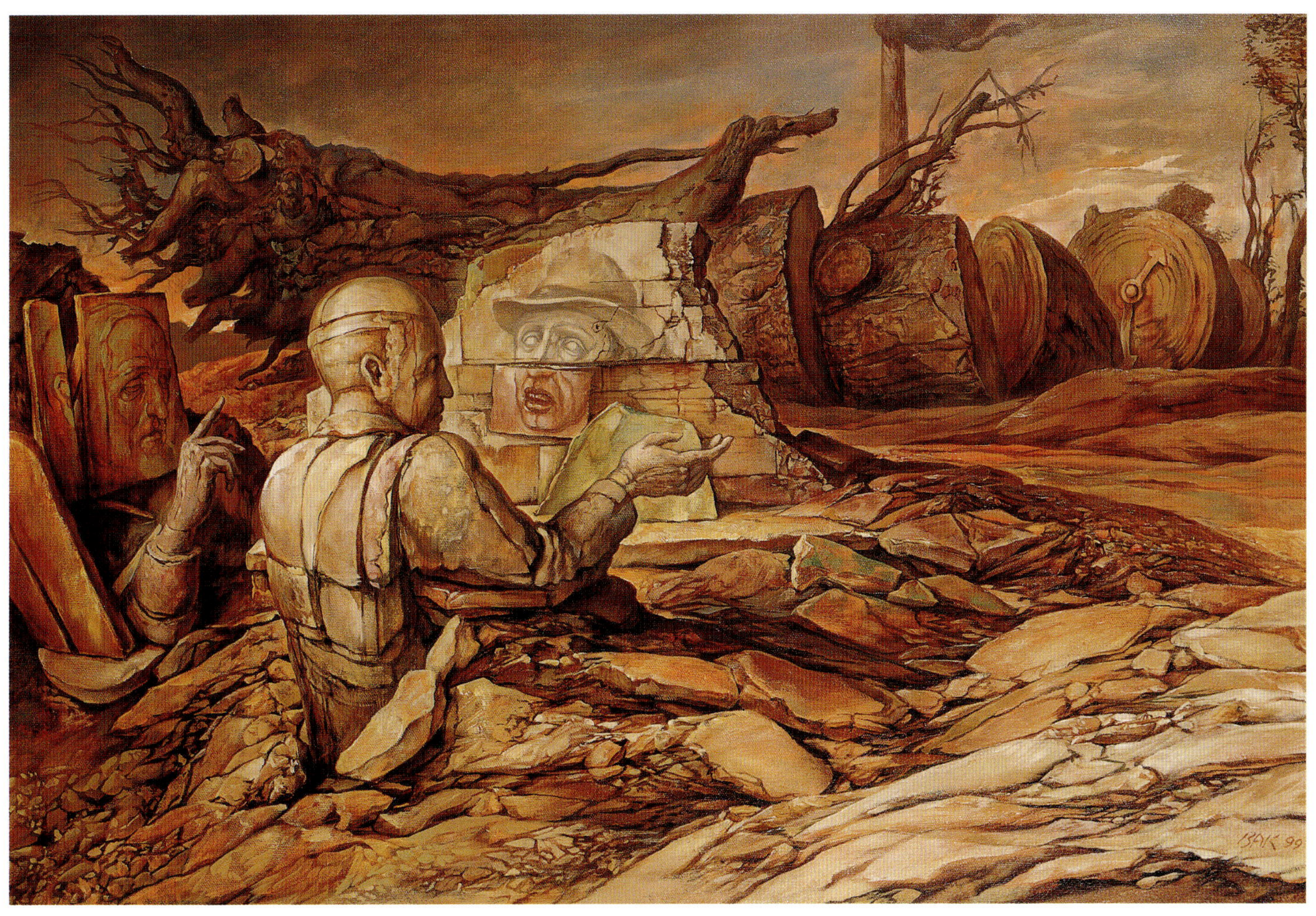

About Time, 1999
Oil on canvas, 20 x 30"

is little more than an outcropping of rock; the human faces before and adjacent to him appear to warn and instruct him about the direction he must take if he is to interpret and repair the ruins of time. Here, as in many of the paintings in this series, biblical and historical vistas collide, and the idea of creation slides into a version of re-creation. The imagination is constantly assaulted by the need to reconstitute its vision of experience using a mixture of ingredients from an ever-changing physical and spiritual reality. Adam's advisors in *About Time* seem to represent an ancient sage and a modern confidant, perhaps a Holocaust survivor, and the challenge before Adam – and before us – is to find a way of reconciling their respective views.

Before one can "be" what was seen, one must first see what has been. Bak's paintings demand a seeing beyond mere looking, until sight gradually glides into insight, an agenda for internaliz-

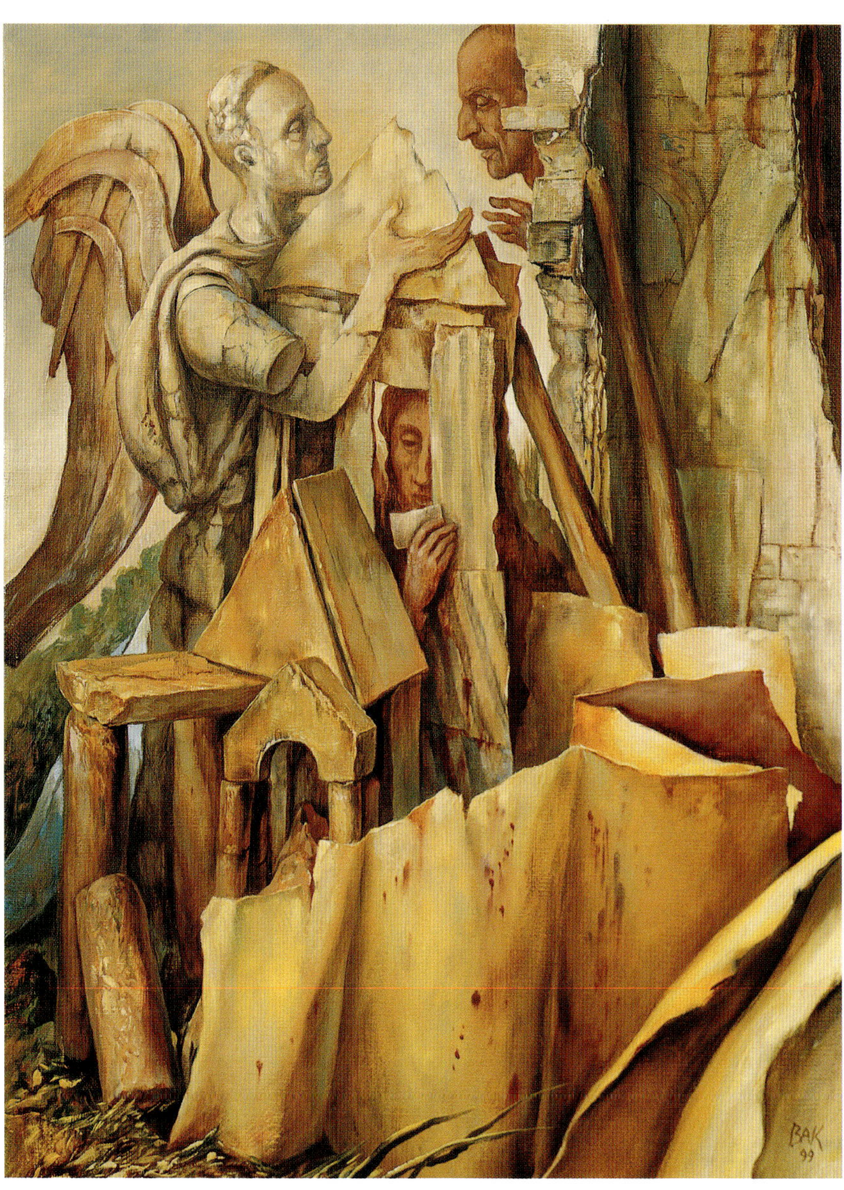

Conversation, 1999
Oil on canvas, 16 x 12"

ing the artistic encounter that helps to explain the process of how one can be what was seen. We first meet the figures in a painting, who possess their own dramatic truth, based on their understanding of what has been. Then we confront the artist's view of his creation, both intentional and subconscious. Finally, we contend with our own perception of both, embracing contradictions where we cannot reconcile them and often struggling to accept an ultimate ambivalence that may be contrary to our expectations about the role of art in its representation of the human scene. Another related group of canvases from *In a Different Light* challenges our sense of "knowing" by enacting in their very content the disputes between tradition and modernity, faith and skepticism, the disruptions of history and the certitudes of eternal truth. The silent exchanges in *Conversation* pits a marble angel, more Roman than biblical in appearance, against a human face emerging from a brick structure that could easily be the remnant of a crematorium chimney. A monumentalized past greets the ruins of the present and leaves us wondering whether any mutual basis for discourse can be found. The key image is in the painting's center, the partially obscured solemn face of a camp inmate, touching the fragment of cloth that was once his prison garb. For the moment his memories eclipse the talk above his head. How can this messenger of God defend himself against the account of destruction that will fall from his interlocutor's lips? Will a time come for the Holocaust too when monuments will be the only vestiges of its terrible history? Will the future one day provide a pillar shape for the chimney equivalent to the columns that link the angel to a holier edifice, the makeshift temple that we associate with his own fragmentary form? Or will the memory that the survivor clings to resist efforts to monumentalize the evil of annihilation, acknowledging that this grotesque parody

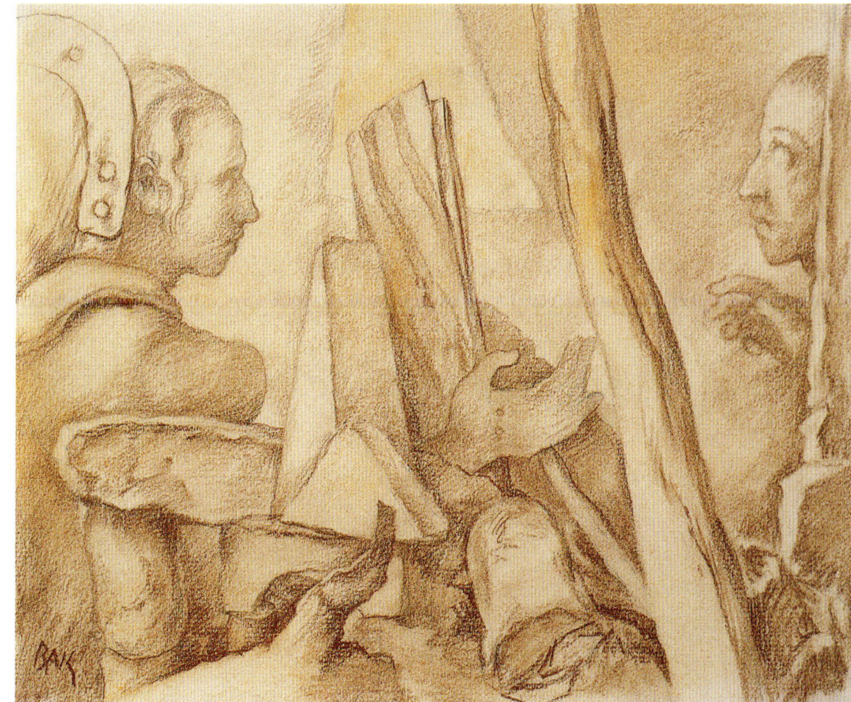

Study for Conversation, 1999
Crayons & pastel on paper, 9 1/4 x 11 1/2"

of angelic influence in human affairs will never find a visual equivalent to restore equilibrium to its intrinsic disarray. In many ways Bak's paintings pay tribute to the countermonument movement in modern Germany, where many architectural attempts to commemorate the event we call the Holocaust have shunned the idea of public memorials that project order and hence consolation in their conventional designs.

Bak's *Day and Night* clarifies some of these issues. Against the background of countryside ravaged by fire Bak constructs a domestic façade that fails to conceal the conflagration, or to hinder the eye from entering into its devastation. Its reality seems to have eroded much of the substance of the angelic figure guarding the entrance to the scene of the disaster. Despite its raised palm that former spiritual deputy now full of vacant space seems powerless to prevent the solitary traveler, perhaps a deportee surrounded by his meager belongings, from penetrating the blazing landscape to meet his fate. Beyond the façade looms a crucifix, once the herald of salvation, which has been drawn as a gallows, a harbinger of death. The traveler is totally oblivious to the ghostly messenger from heaven, whose contours deconstruct before our eyes. The indifference of flesh to spirit resembles the opposition between day and night. The man seems puzzled rather than solaced by the fallen wing beside him. The rungs of the ladder offer descent as an alternative to ascent, but it is not a hopeful option and certainly no means of escape. The melange of imagery is held together by slender threads of sense, as if the whole edifice of fractured shapes were about to topple in the absence of solid foundations to prop it up. We experience the dearth of sturdy forms as testimony to the disappearing unity once celebrated by the symbols of transcendence

Daylight and nighttime themselves are tainted by the pink and purplish shades that dominate this canvas. We are faced with a reflected incandescence, as the main sources of illumination are hidden from view. Lacking a familiar internal principle of structural coherence such as a conventional commemorative monument might possess, *Day and Night* stimulates the consciousness and imagination of the viewer to embrace a cardinal principle of art associated with the Holocaust – in representing this painful theme the act of creation must contain in its vision of the human scene some evi-

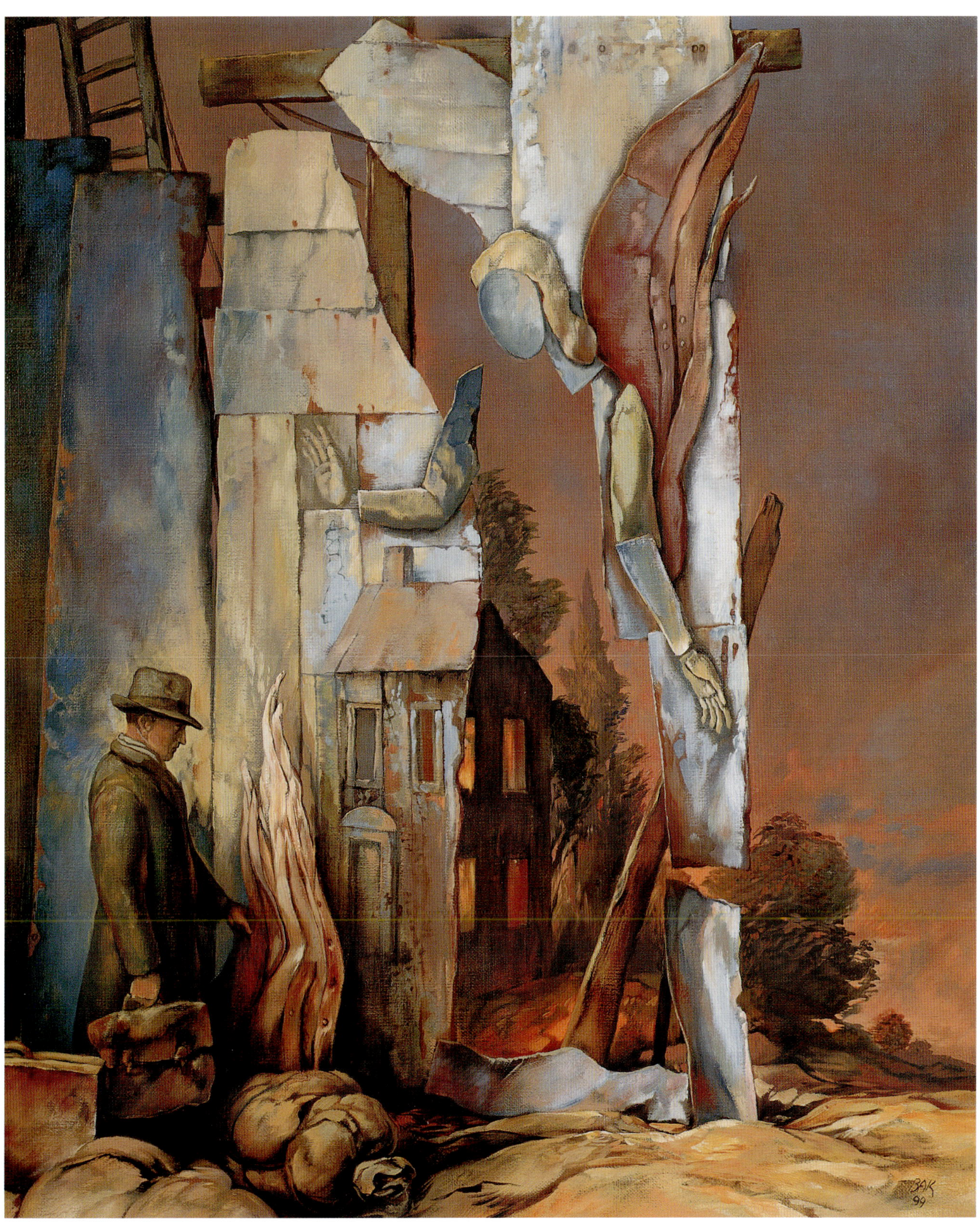

Day and Night, 1999
Oil on canvas, 22 x 18"

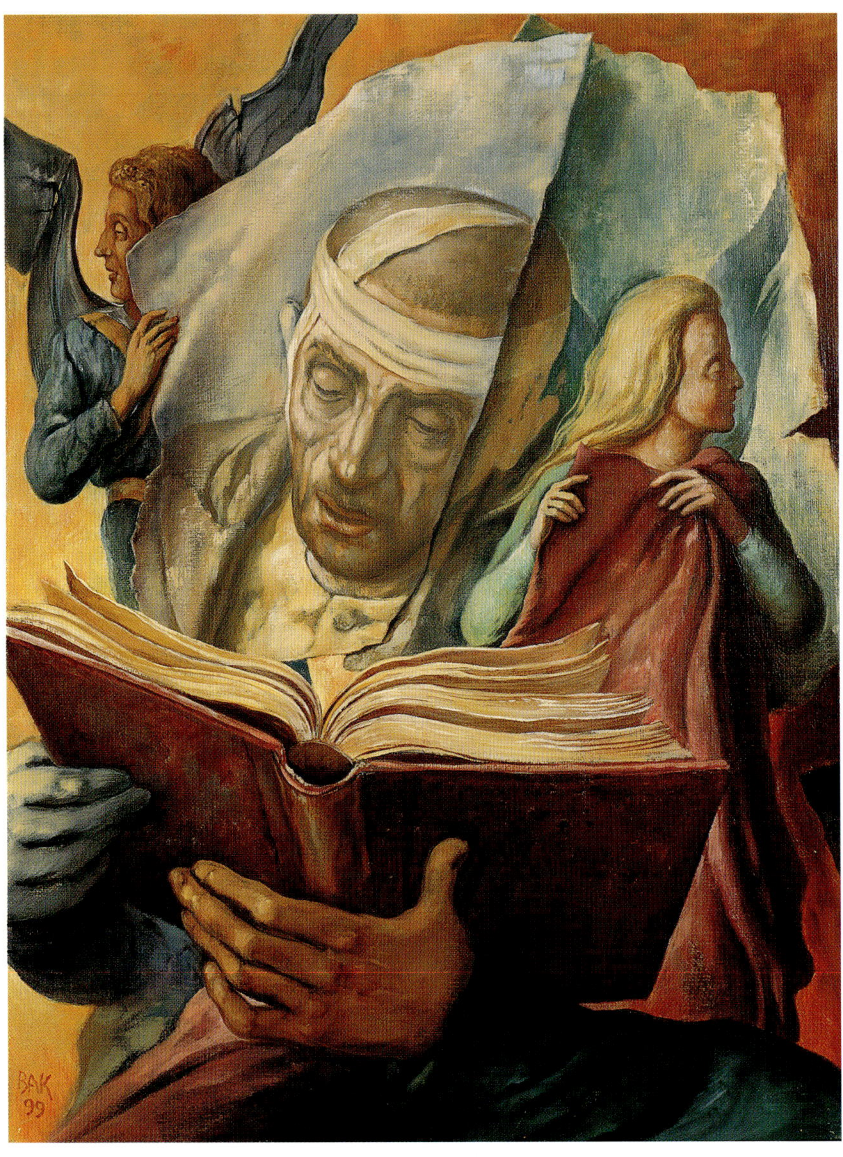

Reading, 1999
Oil on canvas, 16 x 12"

dence of the deed of destruction too. Form and chaos, longing and disillusionment thus vie for our regard, the resulting tension invading us with an anxiety and sense of turmoil that are twin legacies of the subject to which Bak devotes so much of his artistic energy.

The portrait of the wounded self in *Reading* reflects this desperate stress. It is not clear whether the angels are shielding the human figure or themselves from the blazing background, as if both he and they were striving to avoid its encroaching threat. One has the sense that these ministering angels with averted eyes and doll-like features serve outmoded roles, since the man's attention is fixed on the pages of the volume before him. We are not privy to its text,

With a Hidden Face, 1999
Crayon & pastel on paper, 25 1/2 x 19 3/4"

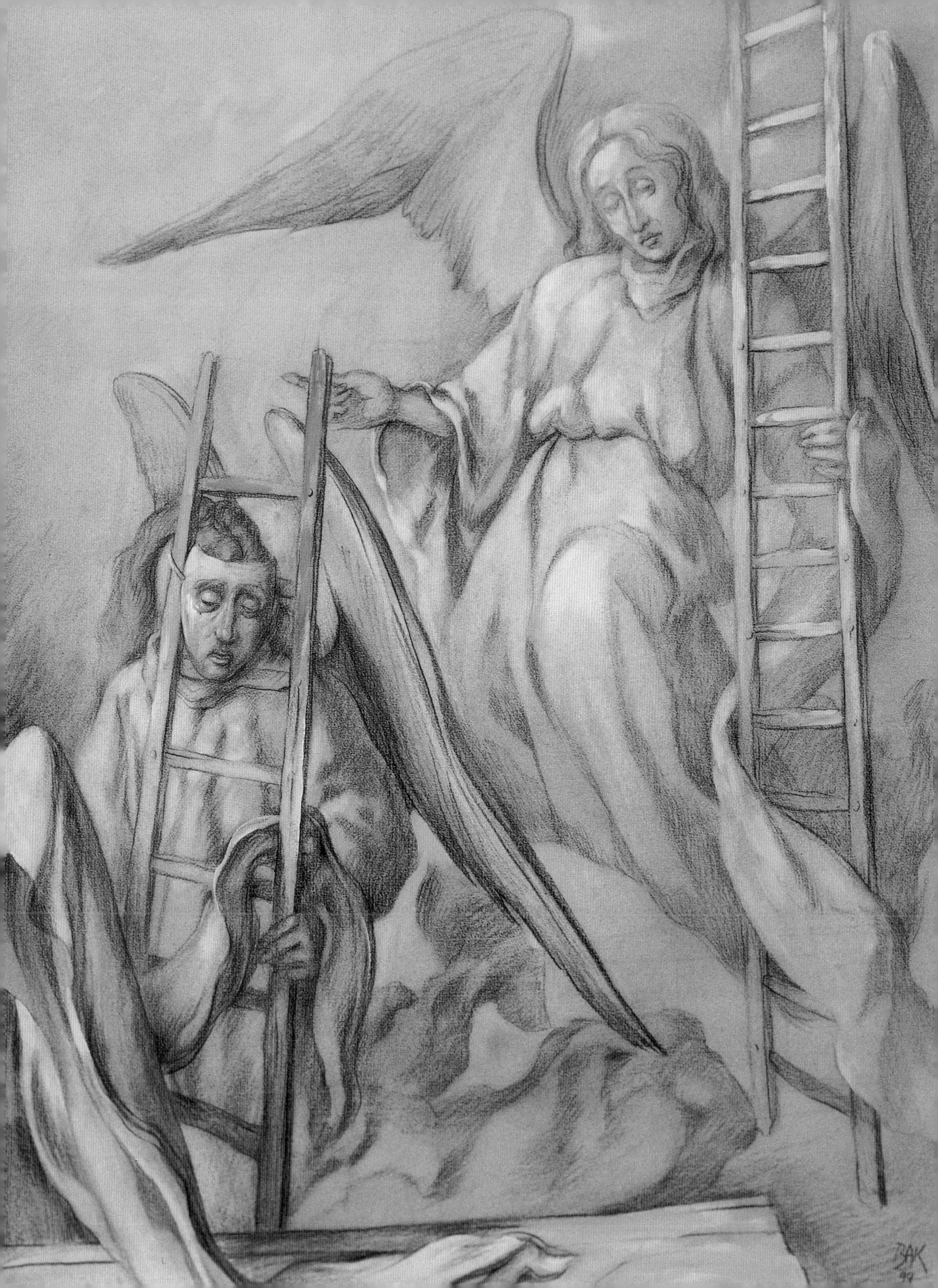

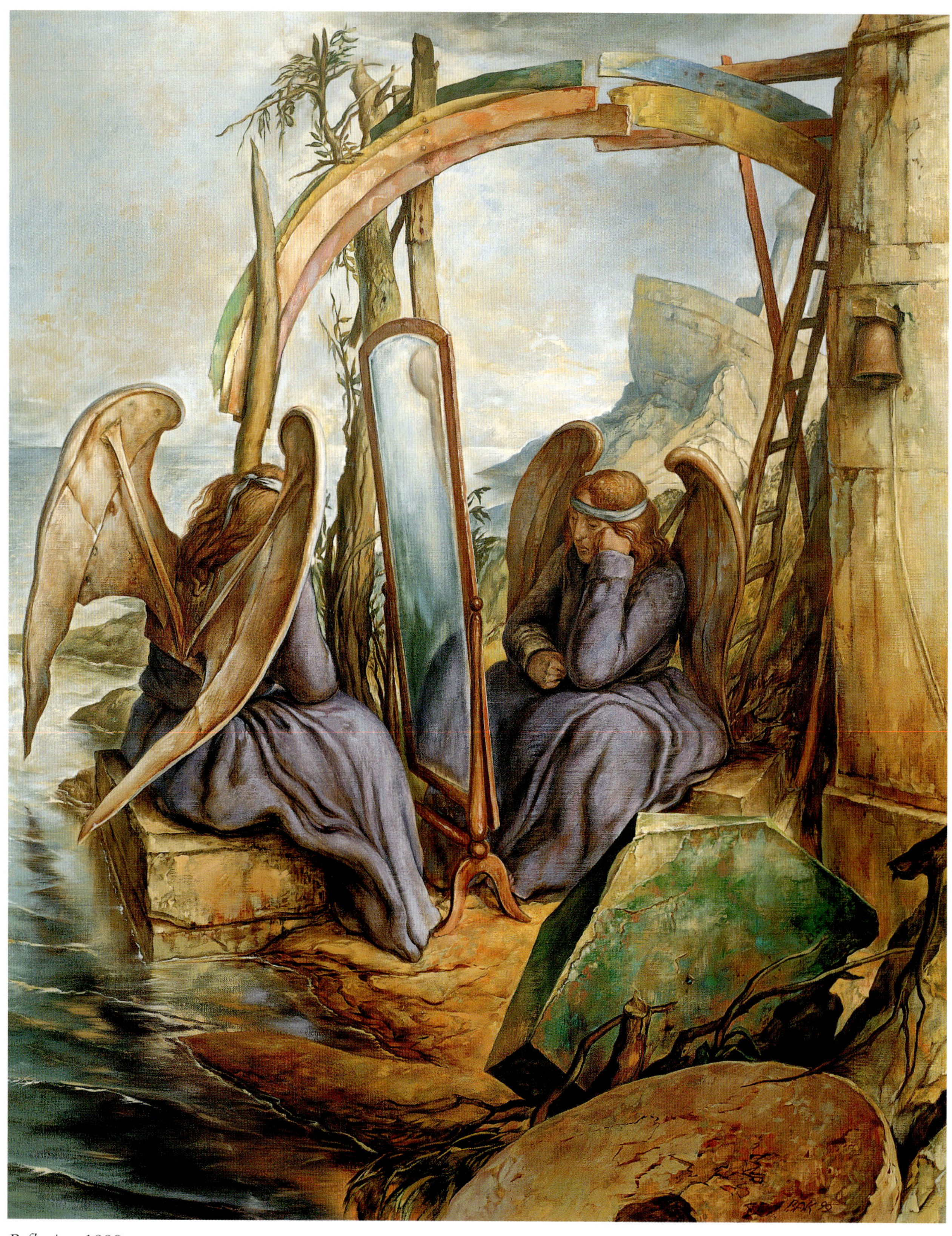

Reflecting, 1999
Oil on canvas, 40 x 32"

nor whether he is seeking an explanation of past events or a means of regaining a secure future. One hand is rendered with glowing tones of healthy flesh, the other with the ghastly tints of a corpse. Is he in frantic search of the clue to renew his spiritual heritage, or merely praying for a way to escape the invading flames? He is poised in space, well into the text, far from the moment when, as in Michelangelo's version, God and the angels conspired to turn the inanimate Adam into a living creature. That divine formula seems to have been reversed, as the children of Israel are now wounded and slain, while the human mission in a divinely ordained world has gone astray. Whether Hebrew Scripture or some other volume contains the solution to the mystery of our errant heritage, the viewer is left to decide.

One of the few anomalous themes of *In a Different Light*, highlighted by *Reflecting*, is the dilemma of the angels, laid-off actors in the drama of God's universe who are left to ponder the reasons for the loss of their usual employment. They are poised on a promontory surrounded by the waters that once, as a sign of God's displeasure with His creation, drowned all living creatures with the exception of Noah and the voyagers on his ark. They seem pensive and disconsolate, gazing into opposite sides of a pier glass that mirrors the double entendre of the painting's title. They meditate on their own images as if wondering what to do next, like stranded messengers cut off from any possibility of completing their intended mission. Seated beneath the arching remnants of a proverbial rainbow, a breached semicircle deprived of its luminous promise, they portray the dilemma of a world that appears to have lost contact with its heavenly source. Their princely purple robes are sad but vivid reminders of their erstwhile task, the earthbound ladder behind them a diminished echo of the spiritual purpose they once pursued between the human and the divine. Is the longing for a semblance of their former selves a sign of angelic nostalgia or a disenchanted critique of our surrender to the illusion that once infused them with vital meaning?

Although Bak usually exercises great restraint in his treatment of the angelic theme, one drawing seems to explode with bitter irony at the paradoxical notion of a tormented world still under the protection of angelic influence. In the drawing

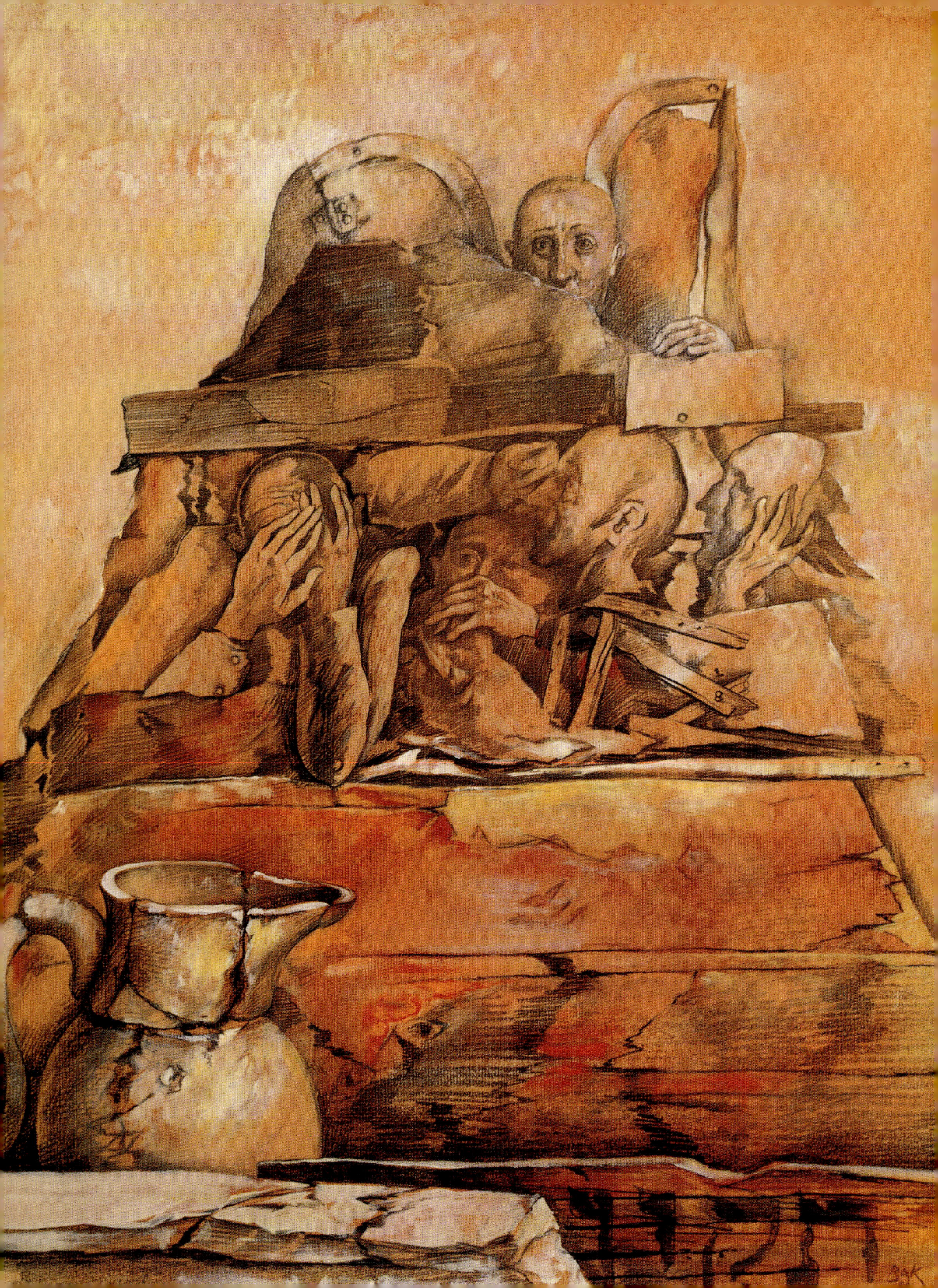

Under an Angel's Wings a pained angel becomes a victim himself, as he is unable to relieve the burden crushing the grief-stricken faces beneath him. The irony is intensified by the carefully organized geometric design of the drawing, its spatial composure forming a tense contrast with the compressed anguish squeezed between its frames. There is a Goya-esque terror in the twisted bodies before us, while the bloodstained surface in the foreground minimizes the "still life" from which the cracked pitcher is borrowed and promotes instead the "still death" of a new post-Holocaust artistic tradition. Both art and spirit must pay a price for the near triumph of mass murder, and one of the most singular and provocative inferences of Samuel Bak's vision is that art seems to have made the quicker recovery. Here we see what exists under an angel's wings, and there is nothing holy about it; whatever hovers above them, if anything, is lost in missing space.

What occupies that missing space is not always a matter for speculation. A drawing in crayon and oil called *Study for an "Encounter*"*, and the painting based on it, *Encounter**, give us a glimpse into how Bak's works continually challenge the viewer to search for suppositions beyond the perimeters of the picture. In *Encounter* a grieving woman extends a hand and finger in a gesture once reserved for the moment of creation. Now, it seems, she would be grateful for any kind of contact. Whether she is pointing or pleading we do not know, but her raised forearm appears suspended in expectation of a reciprocal sign. The human figures beside her retreat into an easel that already contains a fading replica of a faceless angel, as if movement from reality to representation confirmed Bak's belief in the vital role of art in a post-Holocaust world. The large single die beneath the vanishing angel-image suggests that chance may have supplanted divine guidance as the arbiter of man's fate. The subject of dispute during the "encounter" may be speculative in the painting, but in the drawing, which is more expansive, the cropped brick structure now is visible as the signature chimney whose twin stacks emit columns of smoke. Surely the topic of discussion is what the people in the painting have survived. While the woman is a solidly sculpted creature of flesh, the fading angel seems partly obliterated by what it hears. This view is supported by the grotesque shape in *Angel**; the

*page 55
*page 54
*page 56

Under an Angel's Wings, 2000
Crayon & oil on paper, 23 3/4 x 19"

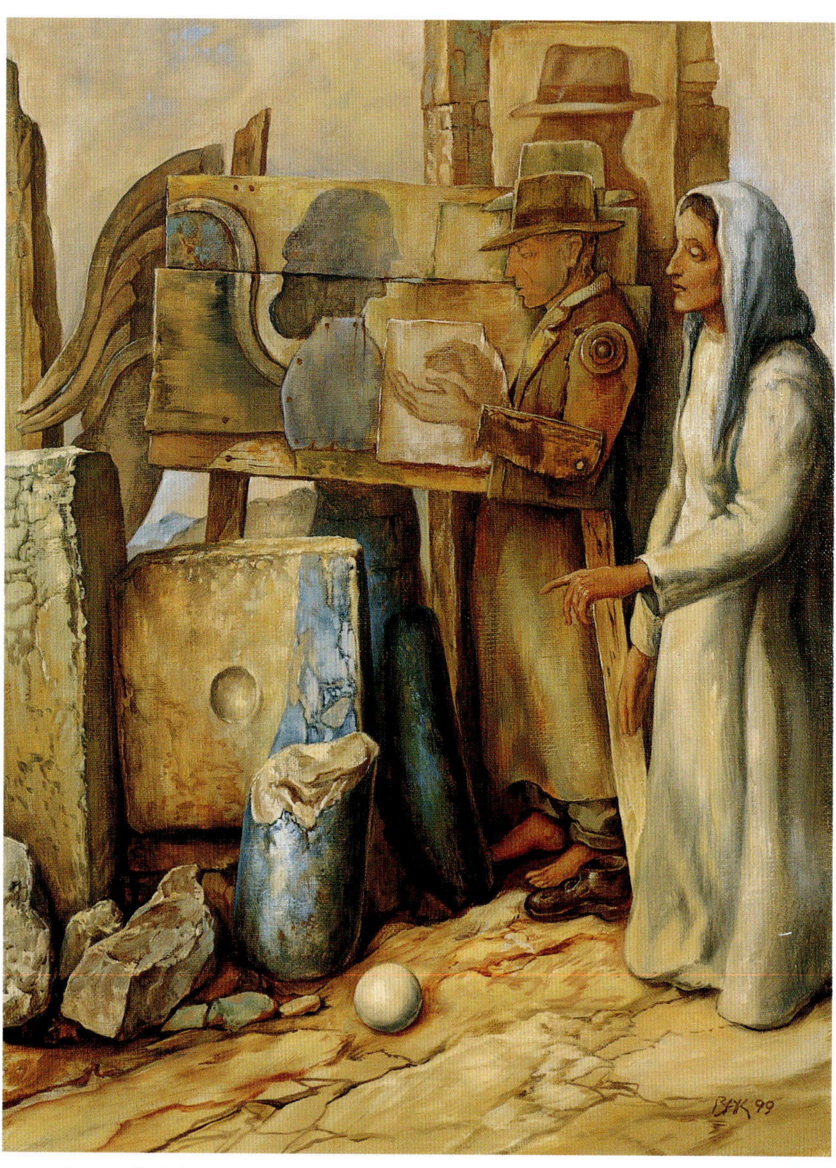

Encounter, 1999
Oil on canvas, 16 x 12"

problem of delineating, not to say imagining, the spiritual essence of the universe grows more and more difficult in the presence of images of destruction like the crematorium chimney.

The desire to reenter that lost realm of the spirit is a natural impulse, and Bak acknowledges it in a whole cluster of paintings from *In a Different Light*. But between the impulse and its realization lies the shadow of mass murder, and the possibility of repairing the rupture that once tore body from spirit may be more than human will can imagine. Indeed, in order to memorialize that disaster honestly, it may be necessary to concede the permanent presence of a void to replace the ancient promise of redemption, at least

Study for an "Encounter", 1999
Crayon & oil on paper, 22 x 15"

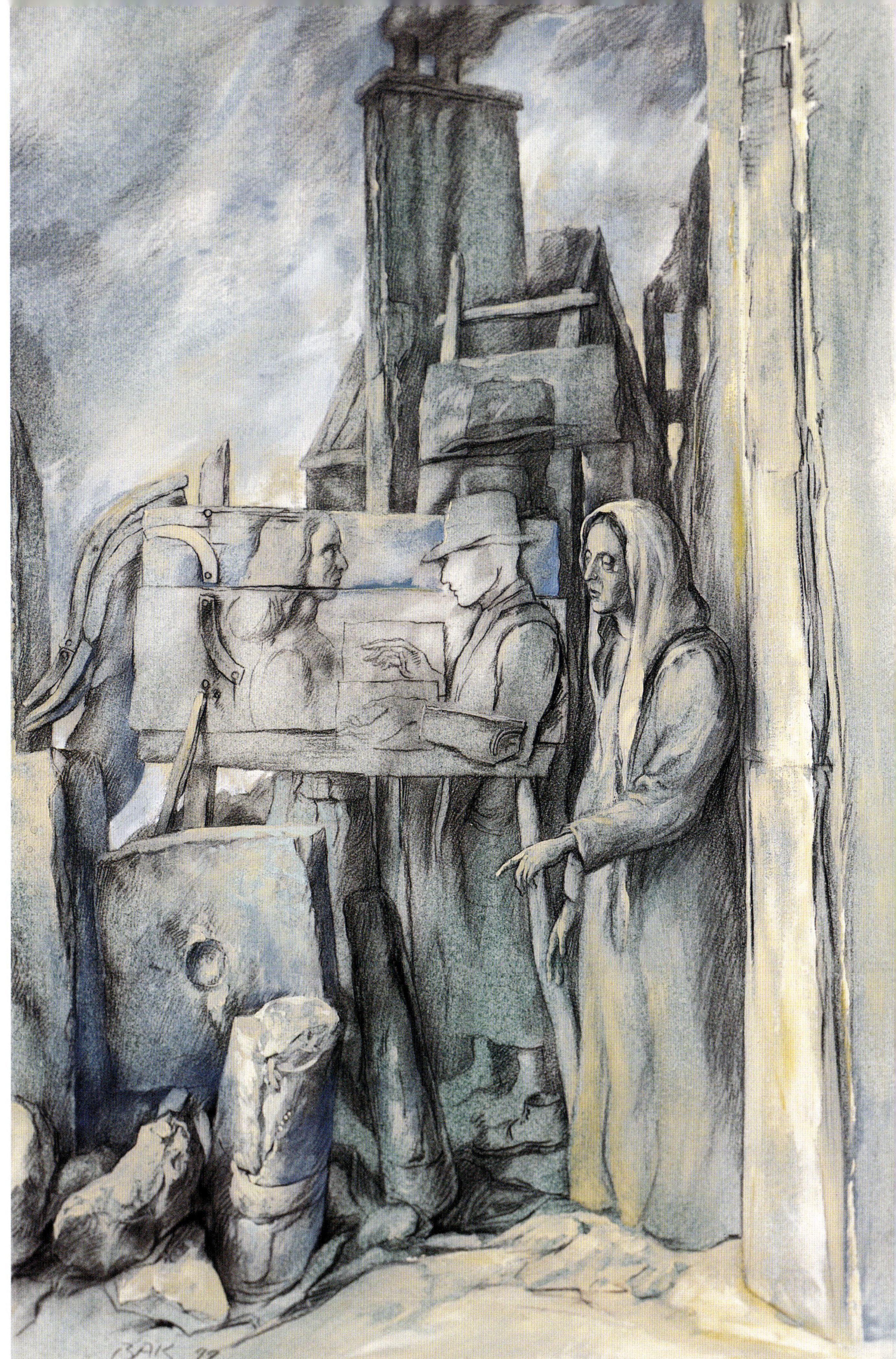

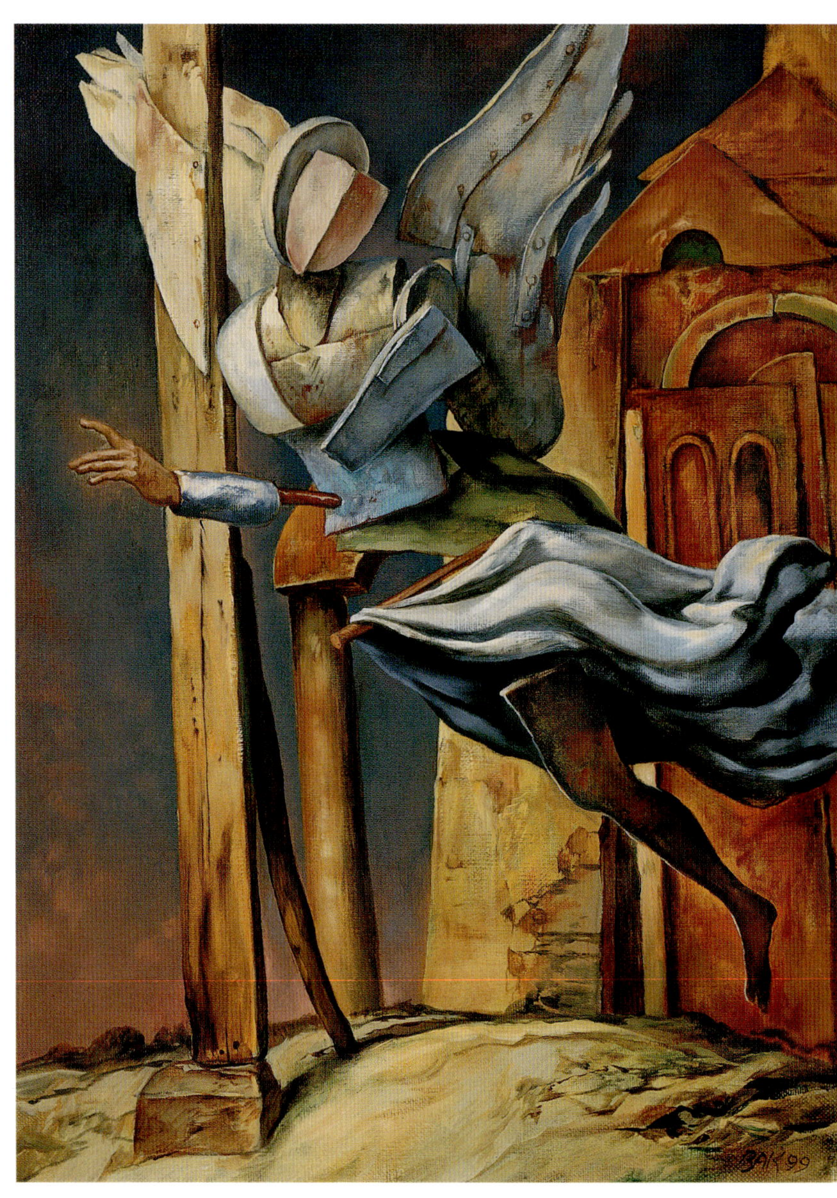

Angel, 1999
Oil on canvas, 16 x 12"

in that part of the human narrative concerned with the Holocaust. In *Cornerstone* the Hebrew letters for the word *tikkun* are built into the flimsy architecture of the landscape. An angel bears a poster-like representation of the last letter, a proclamation from the divine messenger to the weary traveler that his obligation even after sorrows is *tikkun ha'olam*, the mending of the world. But behind the monitory angel's wings looms the emblem of ruin that exerts a force on modern memory far greater than those wings or their metallic replicas clamped futilely to the traveler's shoulders. By including that murderous column as background for this crucial confronta-

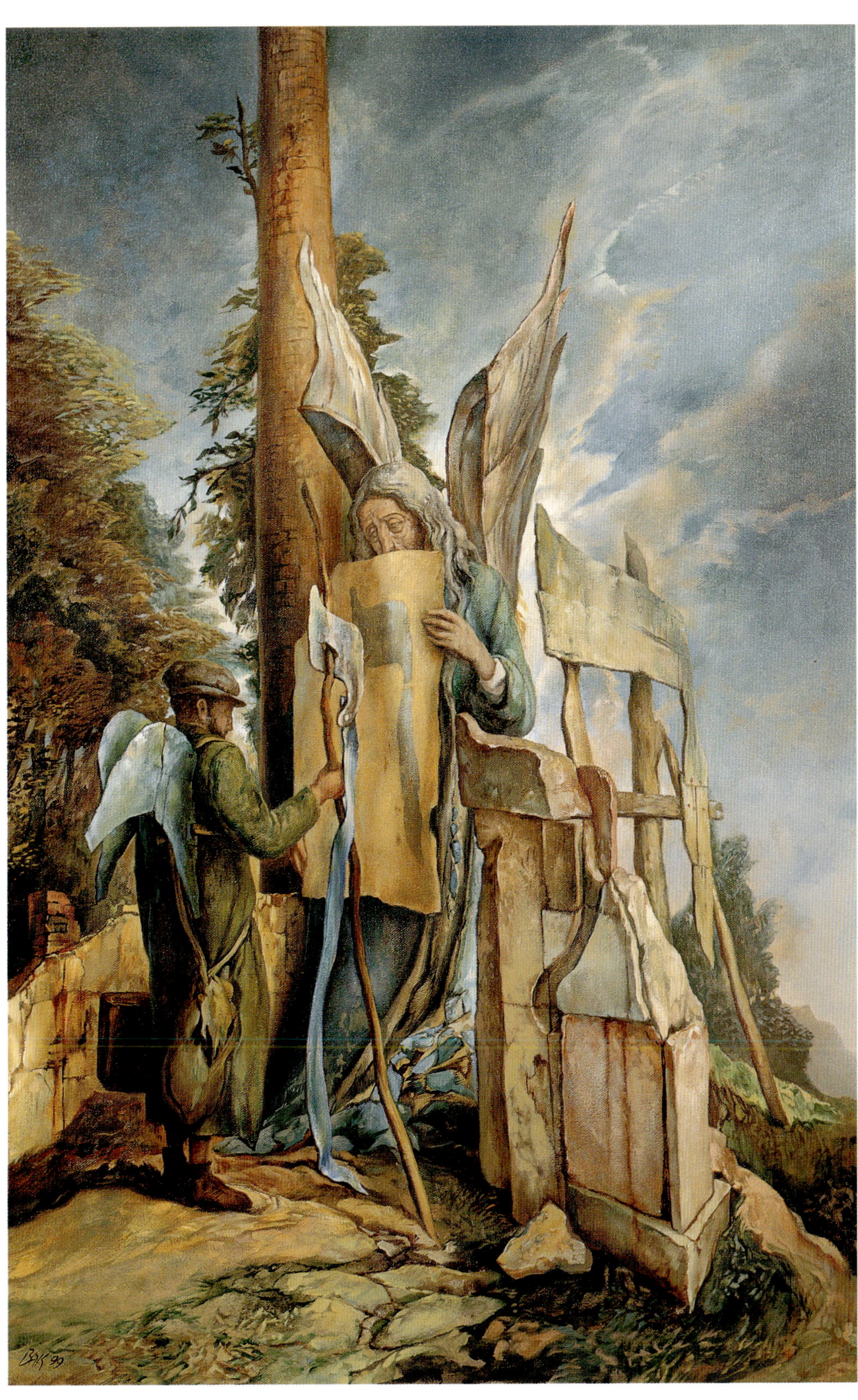

Cornerstone, 1999
Oil on canvas, 30 x 20"

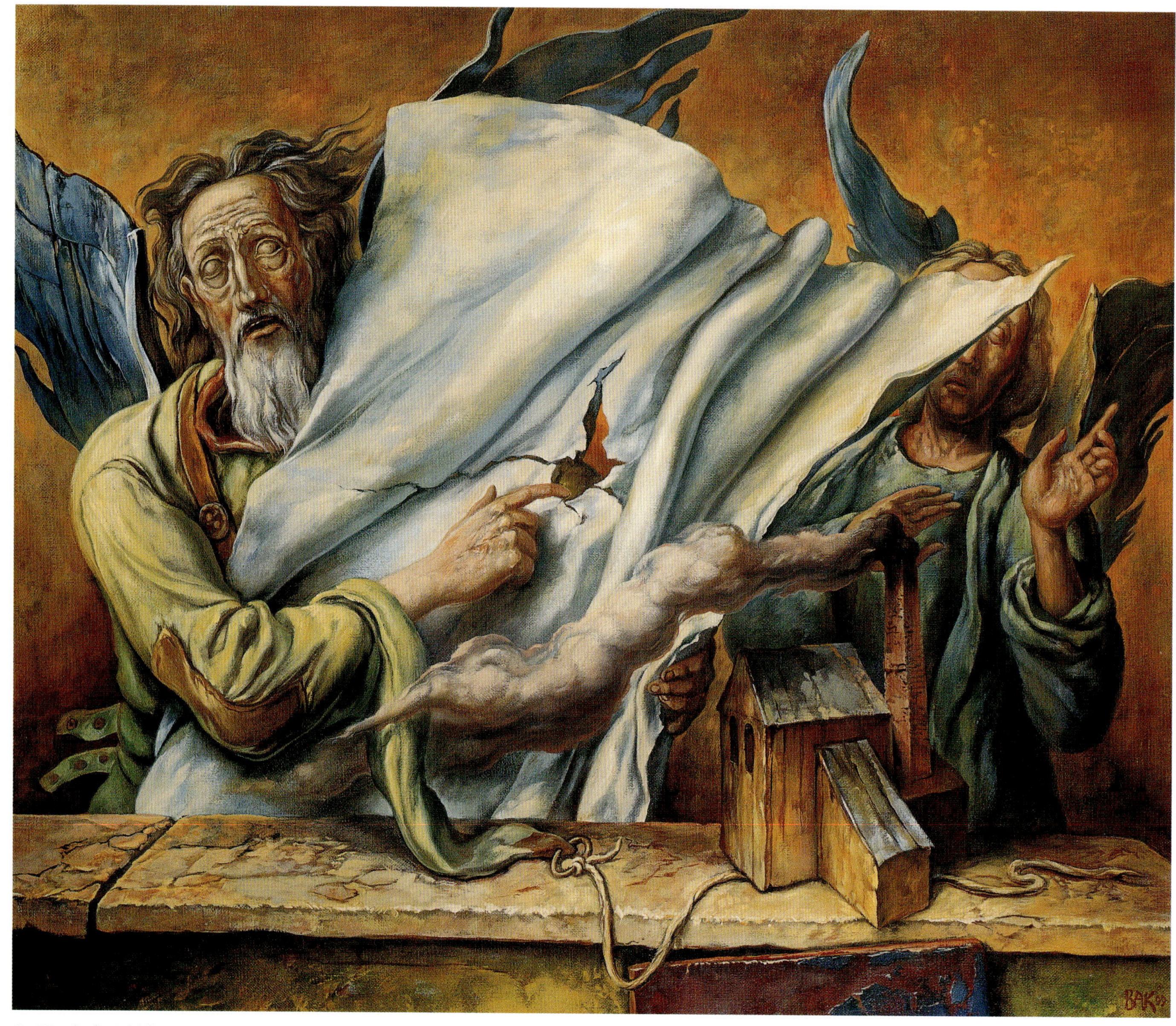

In Need of a Tikkun, 1999
Oil on canvas, 22 x 26"

tion, Bak refuses easy didactic options and leaves the viewer wondering whether the injunction to "repair" may not obscure the impact on modern consciousness of the destruction of European Jewry. At the very least, memory of that carnage sometimes curbs the inclination to repair its wounds.

For the artist, the challenge is to find a panoply of images to convey the enormity of the task, to ask not only how but whether it can be done. *In Need of a Tikkun* presents a winged figure whose visage bears a resemblance to Michelangelo's God, pointing to a rent in a fabric that might well be a large crumpled canvas. On the other hand, when stretched to its full dimensions, it could represent the heavens where once the divine powers reigned. As if troubled by its anomalous proximity, another angelic figure seeks to block the smoke pouring from a tiny replica of a crematorium chimney. In the ongoing saga of divine and human history that began with the moment of Creation, this is not the first tear in the material that theoretically joins time to eternity. Both Bak and Michelangelo find the banishment from Eden central moments in the unfolding saga of mankind. For Milton the lapse (or choice) that led to the expulsion of Adam and Eve echoes in the closing lines of *Paradise Lost*: "They hand in hand with wandering steps and slow/Through Eden took their solitary way." But despite their disconsolate departure we are reassured by the added detail that wherever they choose their place of rest, Providence will be their guide. No such solace lies concealed in the imagery of *In Need of a Tikkun*. Indeed, except for the tiny model of a vacant habitation, no human presence is visible in this painting. The only reply to the divine call for repair issues from the smoke pouring parallel to the pointing hand, but aimed in the opposite direction with the semblance of another finger at its tip. Does it symbolize a mute reprimand from the victims who are no longer able to speak for themselves, to say nothing of joining in the necessary act of repair? Perhaps the tear should remain, as a fixed reminder of a loss that can never be retrieved.

As Far As It Can Go, 1999
Oil on canvas, 18 x 14"

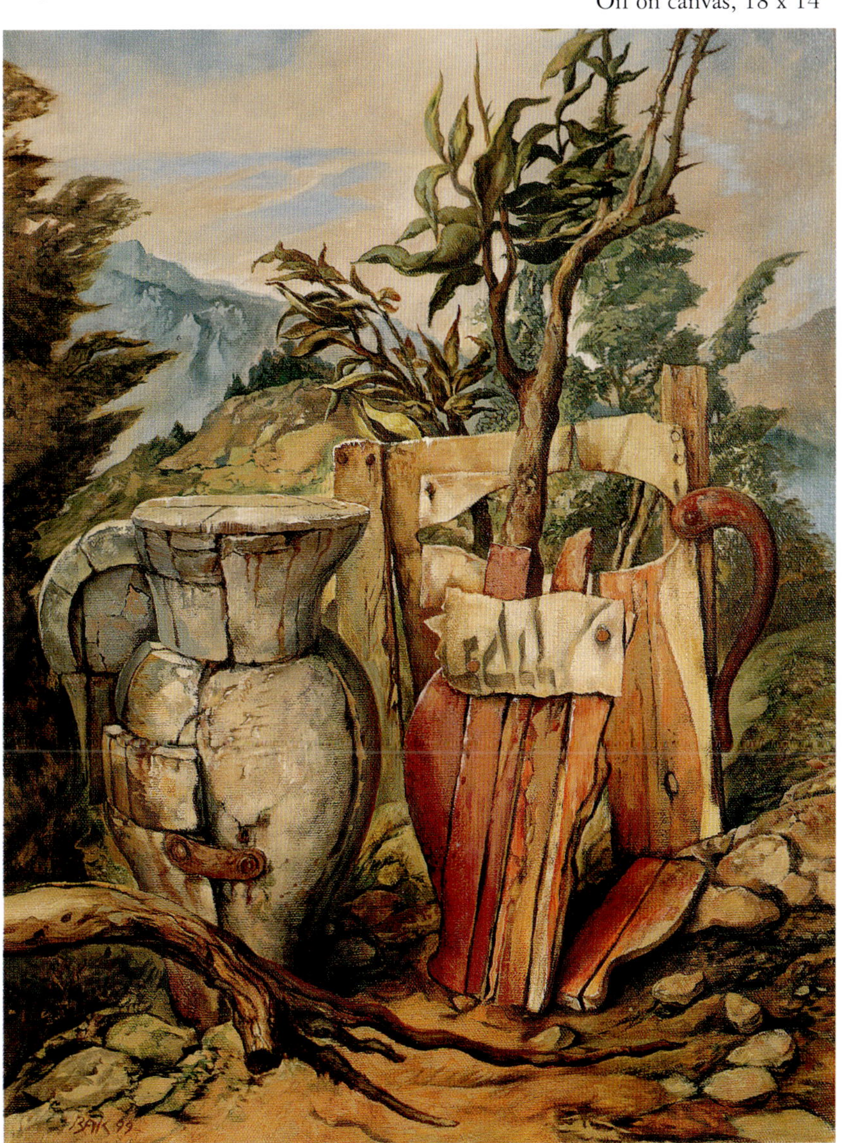

The premise behind *tikkun* is that a successful repair can restore some of the equilibrium lost when a particular disruption of the human community temporarily violates the order implicit in creation. But this is a principle with limitations, as Bak concedes in *As Far as it Can Go**. Here a giant patchwork stone urn reminds us that excavating and reconstructing the past need not reproduce its pristine condition, but only provide us with a damaged and fragmentary version of what had been. The Hebrew letters enjoining *tikkun* are upside down, nailed to a piece of wood, leaning against a rickety gate with its prelapsarian tree that might caution us against trying to recover the lost innocence from that primordial period of an intact Eden. As survivors of the Holocaust slowly pieced together a Jewish world from its European remnants, it became clear to unsentimental observers that the resulting society could never equal its former state. An irreplaceable cultural void lay at its very heart. Thus every depiction of *tikkun* is also a record of what cannot be mended, a paradoxical confirmation

**page 59*

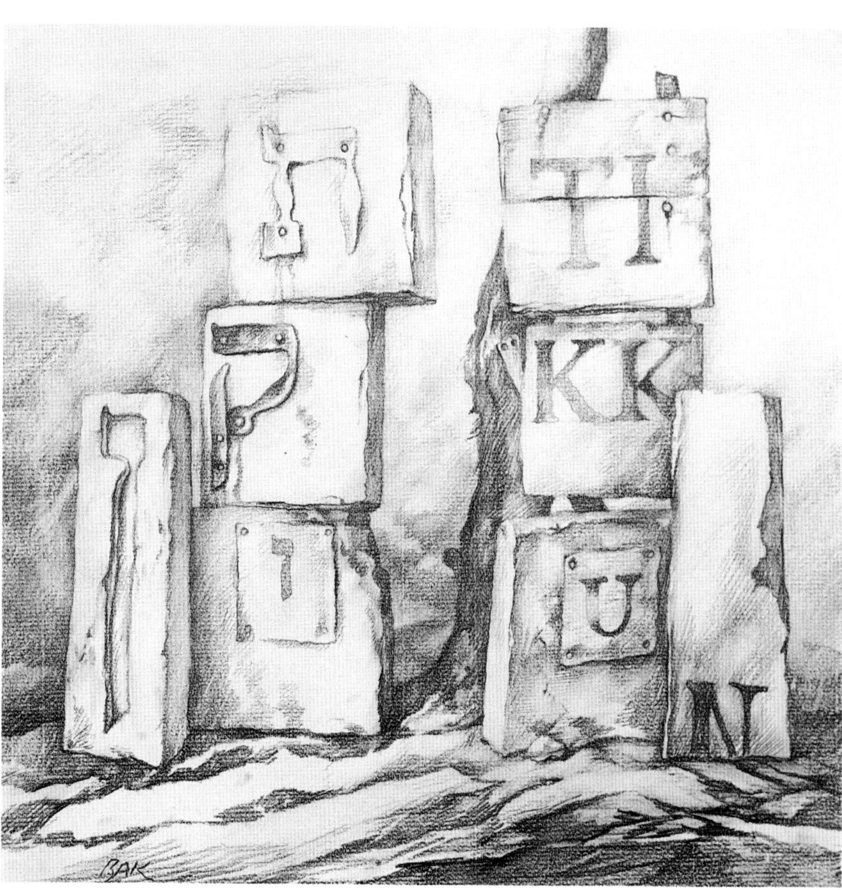

Equivalents, 1999
Pencil on paper, 12 1/4 x 12 1/4 "

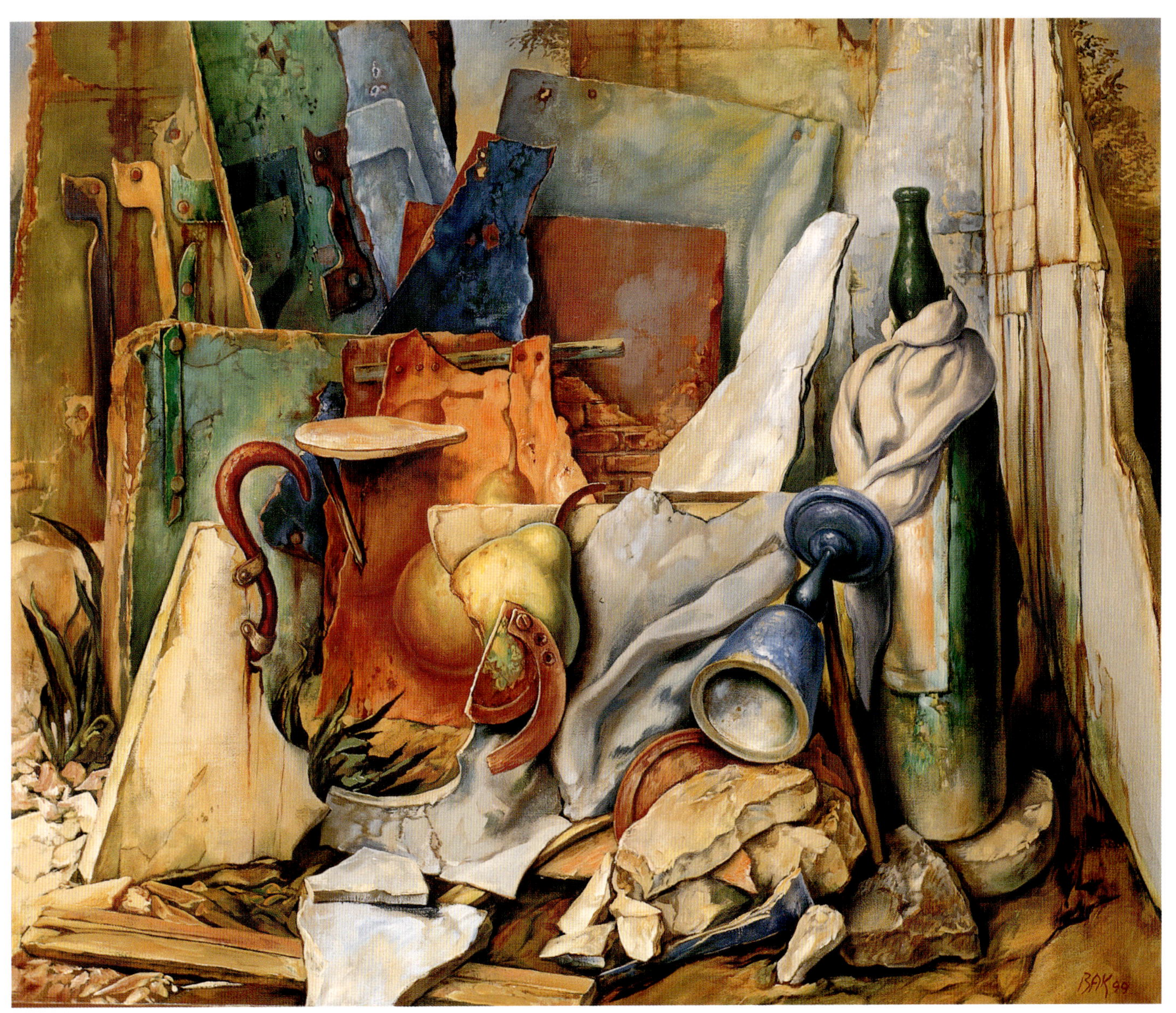

Still Life with Tikkun, 1999
Oil on canvas, 22 x 26"

of the wreckage left behind by a ruin incapable of renewal

Still Life with Tikkun is a serious tribute to an honorable artistic convention, but with a strong tinge of parody. The rich coloration and careful arrangement of forms amidst a chaotic landscape marks Bak as a master of the decomposing composition. His effort to wrest shape from familiar and unfamiliar images, some broken, some whole, reflects the meeting of twin legacies of order and decay. Even the well-known objects found in such paintings assume a different role. The goblet is tipped, filled with empty space, while the

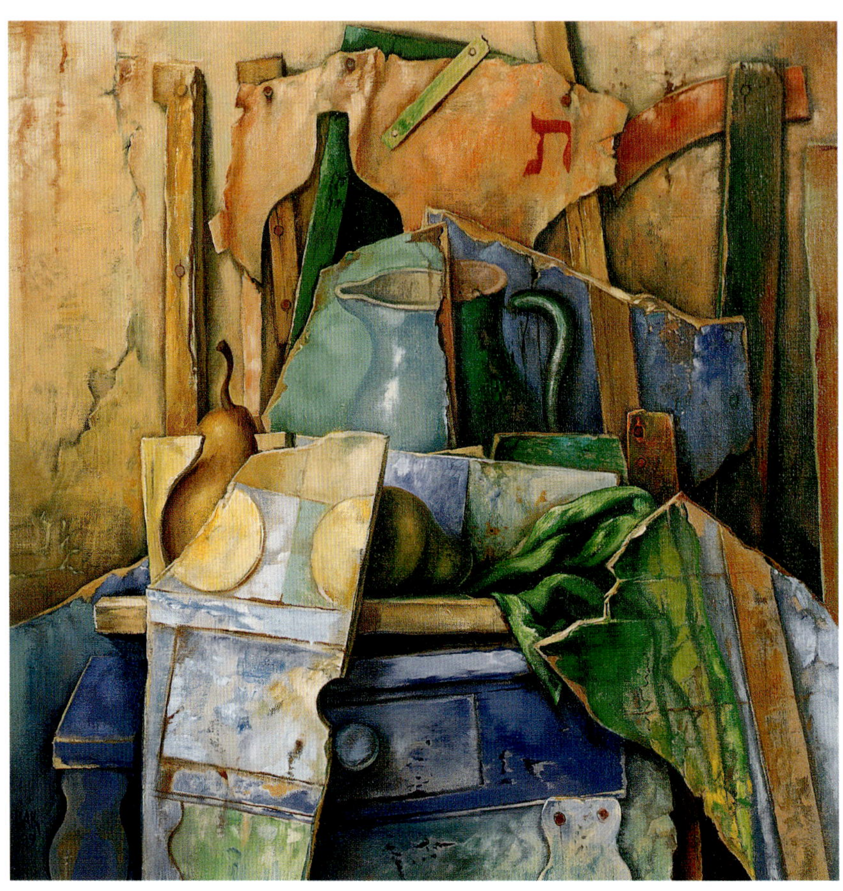

Hidden Tikkun, 1999
Oil on canvas, 15 x 15"

dusty wine bottle with scarved neck suggests another vacant container. Instead of a pair of robust pears we find one half-blocked, the other half-eaten. We are witnesses not to an inviting repast but to a meal hastily abandoned. We are confronted with the spectacle of organized fragments: shards of stone, parts of walls and other structural litter whose brick components echo the inspiration for this testimony to visual ruin. Yet there is an austere and radiant beauty to Bak's vision of decay, which embodies the problem of revising human and artistic traditions without attempting to solve it. The composition absorbs into its content the letters of *tikkun,* which cease to be a guide to conduct and instead are recruited to help enact the aesthetic scene.

Hidden Tikkun and *Still Life* repeat these themes, though each offers fresh perspectives on the view portrayed in their companion canvas. Seen "in a different light," the tranquil domestic "still lives" of earlier artists have been metamorphosed into "stilled lives" tainted by a violence not to be found in their serene prototypes. The pitcher in *Still Life* – the title now betrays a jarring resonance – seems riddled with bullet holes, while the pear, punctured by a nail, is bleeding from its wound. Bak is committed to a technique of indirect entry into the world of the Holocaust. He avoids pictorial representations of its horrors, preferring to prod his viewers to imagine their devastating impact and to face the dilemma of absorbing the remembered havoc unaided by the bracing sensation of graphic delight. The spiritually complex and perilous journey from ruin to restoration is embodied in the difficulty of the transit, a process vividly dramatized by a painting like *The Nature of Roots*,

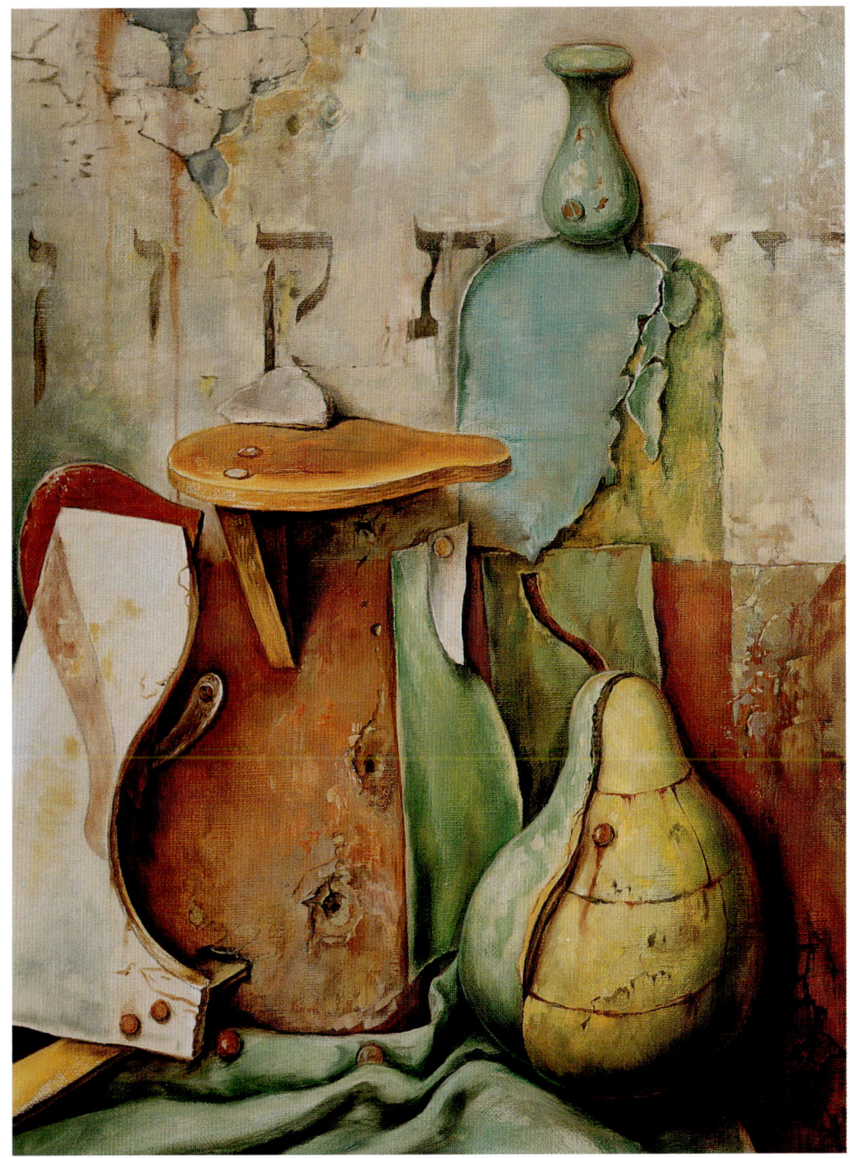

Still Life, 1999
Oil on canvas, 16 x 12"

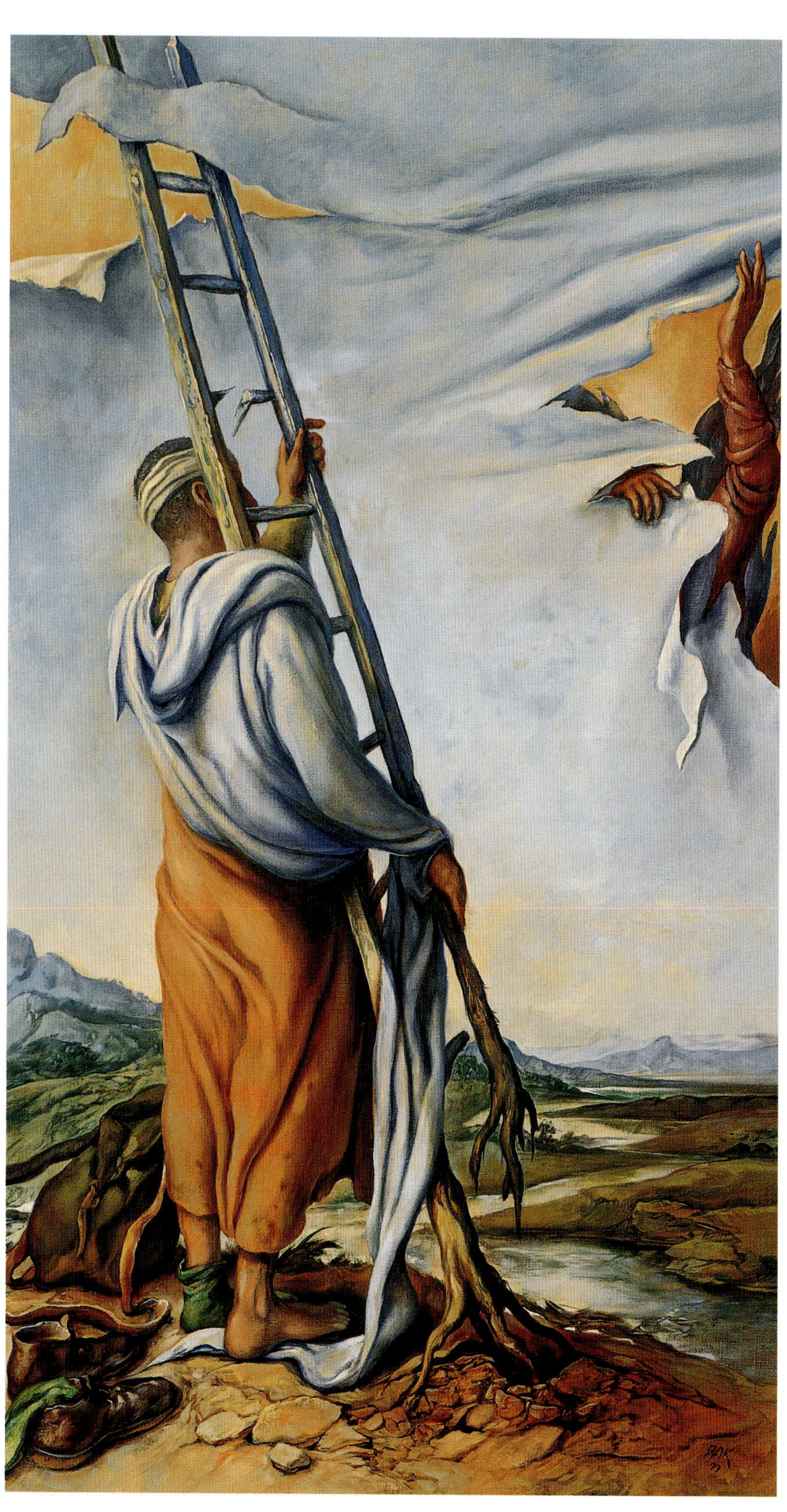

The Nature of Roots, 1999
Oil on canvas, 32 x 18"

where Bak's fondness for fusing disparate materials results in a ladder with tree roots for a base. Here many roles have been transformed. Once it was the nature of roots to plunge deeper into the earth in quest of life-giving moisture. The Jewish equivalent of that pursuit has been brutally severed by Nazi expulsions - a favorite German euphemism for extermination was *ausrotten*, to uproot. But since the putting down of physical roots in a Jewish homeland always implied a spiritual yearning for a heavenly connection, Bak's torn up roots become a ladder raised toward the sky. The damage done below, however, has its parallel in the rent above, a far more portentous injury, since roots are portable, if salvaged in time, in a way that spirit is not. An anonymous angel gestures with the ever-present hand, but who can read accurately its enigmatic signal – if signal it is, and not a hopeless wave of frustration? Meanwhile the featureless ladder-bearer is left to decide how to reestablish a secure foundation of human roots without sacrificing the associate obligation of reaffirming his spiritual origins. The broken rung in the middle of the ladder is a dire omen of the task before him.

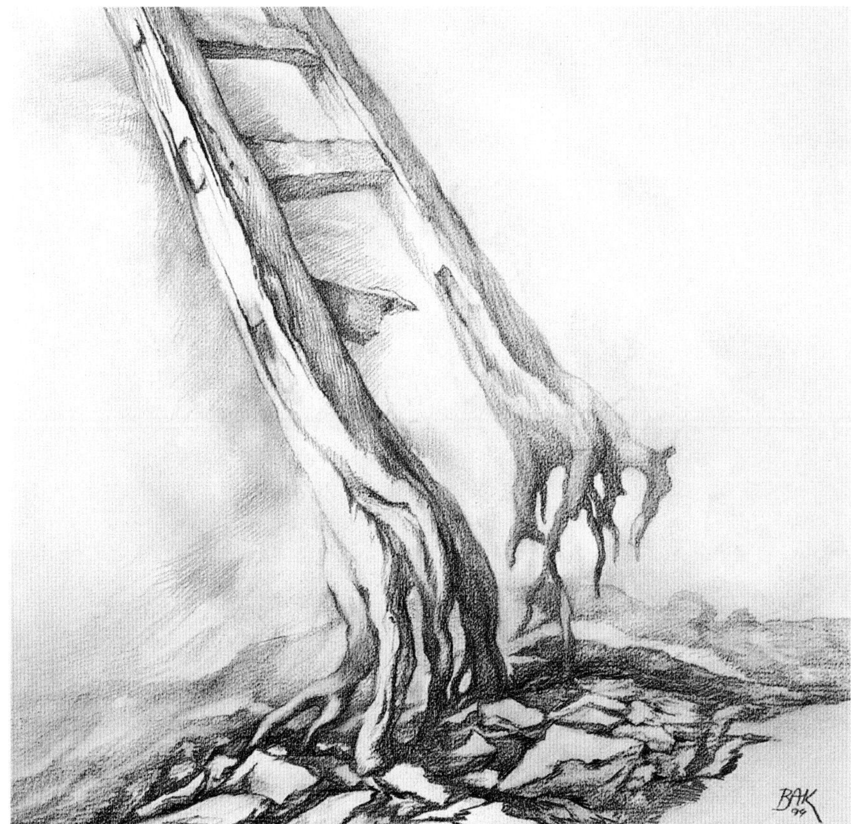

Study for "The Nature of Roots", 1999
Pencil on paper, 12 1/2 x 12 1/4"

The single painting with the simple title of *Tikkun* is an acerbic inquiry into the process, a tribute to organized confusion rather than clarity. The letters of the word preside, upright and inverted, atop a jumble of accumulated rubble. They take the shape of a mountain peak, framed by a bright but cloud-filled sky. As we gaze on this parody of Mount Sinai where once the divine prescriptions for human conduct were presented to Moses, we may recall the shattered tablets that the Lord finally replaced after Moses' intercession for the children of Israel. But when the mutiny of a people is replaced by the murder of innocent victims who require no pardon, even a modern Moses would find little reason to intercede. What then is to be mended, and by whom? Bak's fragile structure is held together only by the strength of artistic form; released from that spell, its components would tumble into the abyss. There is a certain grace to its precarious integrity, but in the absence of spiritual glue to cement the assembly, its unity imparts a successful aesthetic illusion more than a substantive human hope. The articles of domestic use – the broken teapot, the cup and spoon, the cracked vase pierced by the final letter of the word *Tikkun* – seek their own repair. But what of the people who once used them? Implicit in this appeal is the memory of a massive loss; part of its burden is the troublesome question of to whom the obligation to repair should be addressed.

If there is a hint of the subversive in Bak's visual response to this query, an impatience with orthodox solutions, a desire to test our consciousness with the heritage of deprivation we all share, it is nothing more than a frank admission that for him the salves to heal the wounds of Holocaust time have yet to be contrived. This is the theme of *Lost Homes**, where not only the departed Jews but the angel too seems orphaned from his original habitat. He stands behind a ghetto wall, adjacent to a fatal brick pillar: is he the last victim of the disaster that has already consumed the people to whom he once carried messages of divine inspiration? A Bearded Jew with a Christ-like visage but lacking a visible audience, he points to a hole that may be a sign of his own spiritual disrepair. That space may be the void left after the withdrawal of divine presence, but also an indication of the vacuum created when human evil tore the moral fabric of the universe. Whether it represents what the incursions of men have wrought or the deflection of God has allowed, the

**page 68*

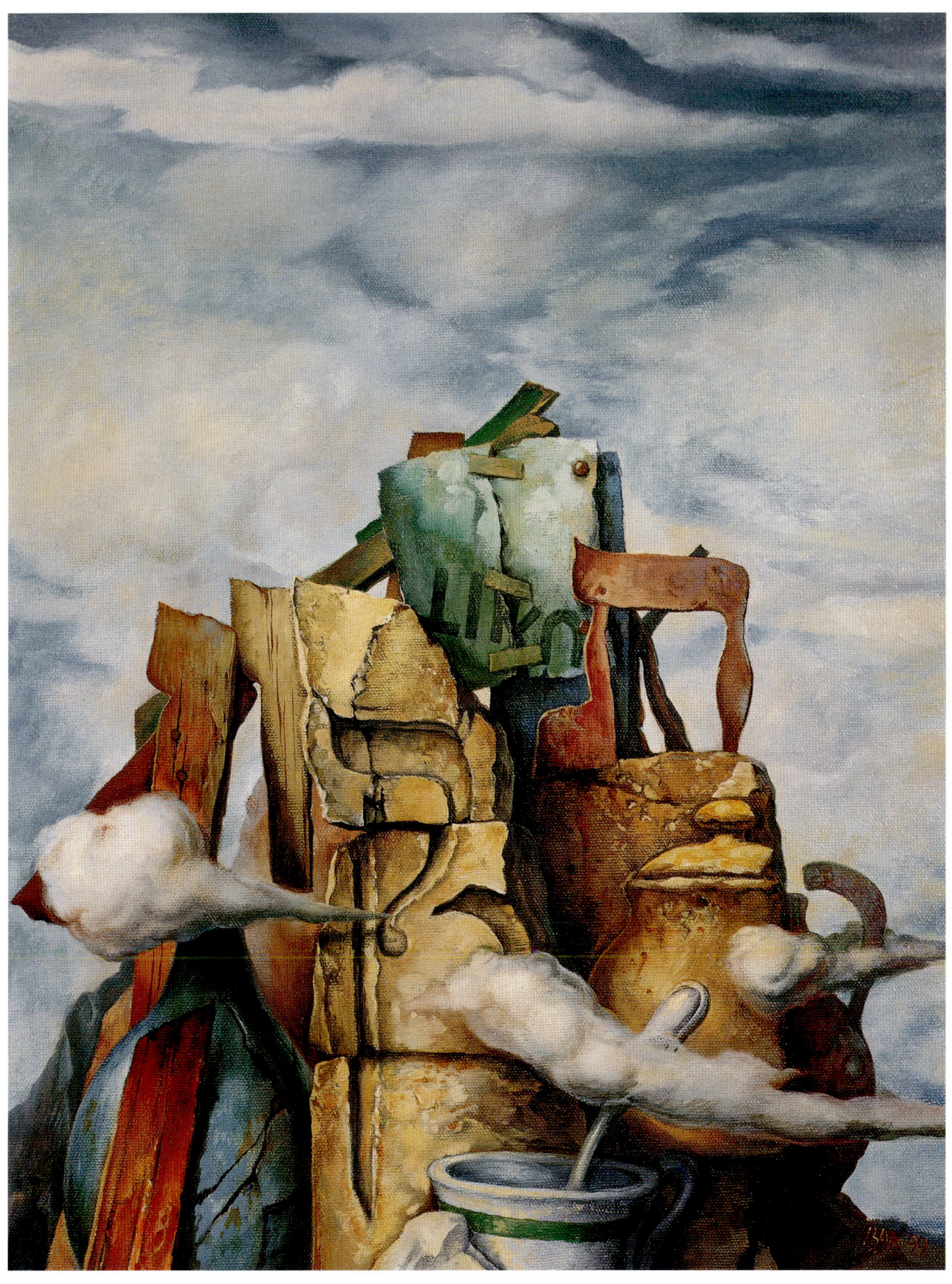

Tikkun, 1999
Oil on canvas
18 x 14"

motif of the hand with extended finger once devoted to acts of creation now imposes on the viewer the responsibility of interpreting the spidery emptiness of its challenge.

The viewer is aided in this endeavor by the cluttered foreground of *Lost Homes*. The telephone pole with its disconnected wires, half gallows and half arrested crucifix, proclaims the temporary triumph of death over resurrection. Those dangling wires touch a sloping roof painted with the gray stripes of the jackets worn by camp inmates. The facades of houses like these are used in many Bak paintings to evoke the ruined Jewish Vilna of his youth.

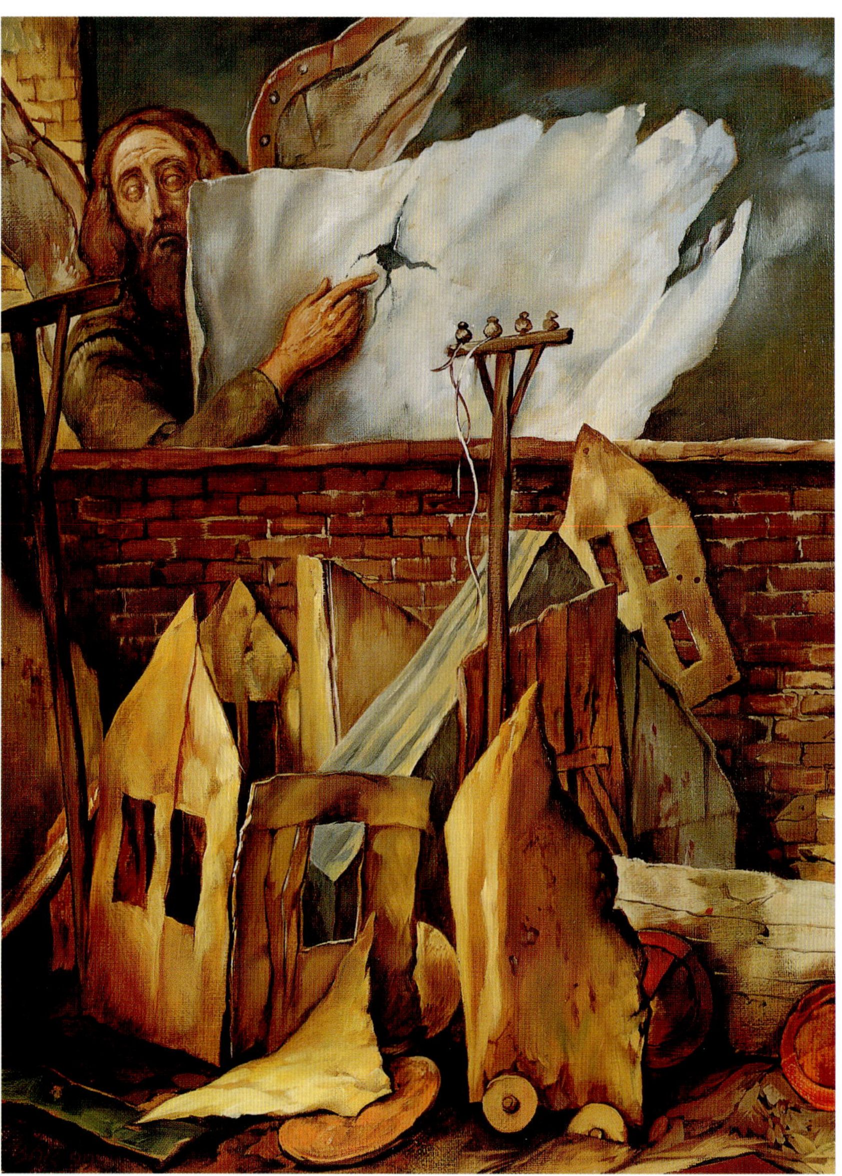

Lost Homes, 1999
Oil on canvas, 16 x 12"

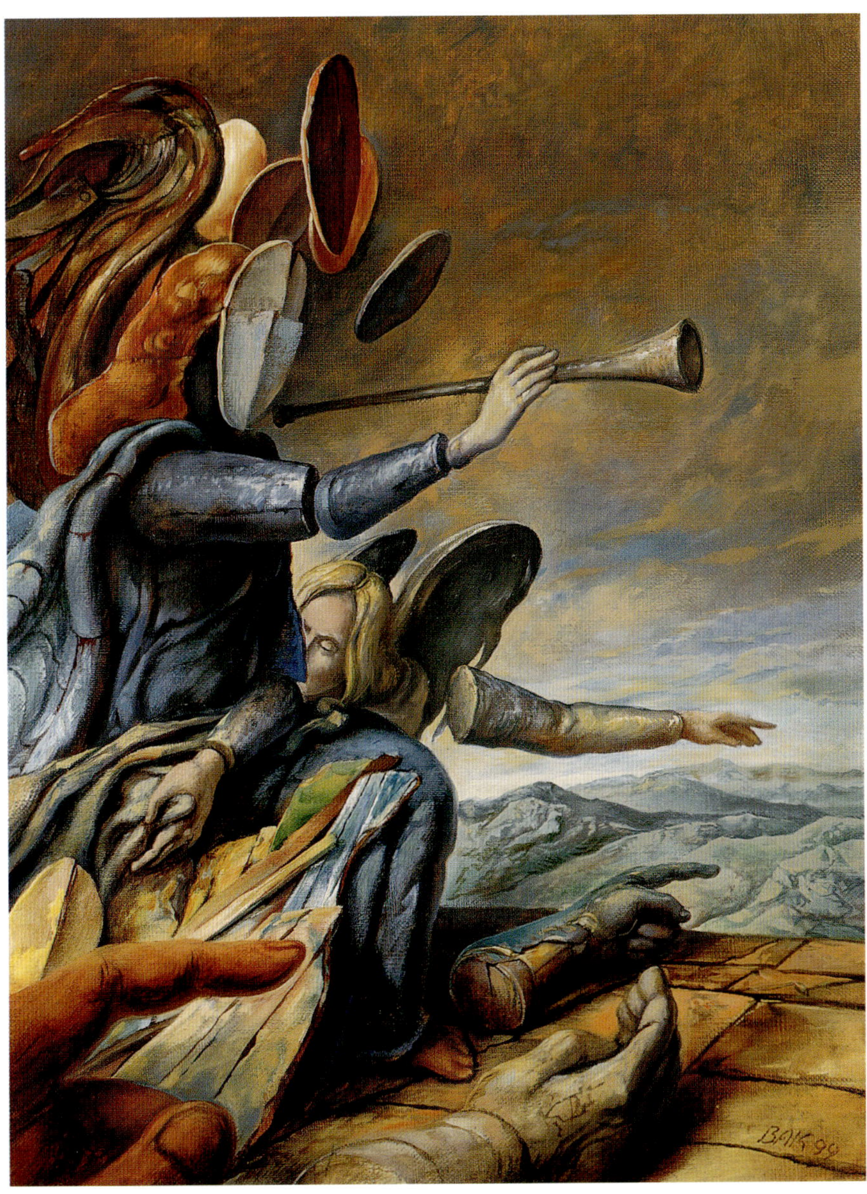

In That Direction, 1999
Oil on canvas, 16 x 12"

Their empty windows stare with eyeless dismay in recognition of a vacancy different from the one to which the angel draws our attention. Were their inhabitants walled in, or walled out, and from what? Are we asked to lament an absent God, or mourn an absent people? The wall appears to loom as a barrier between the two, an image of the hurdle separating death from transfiguration that remains an abiding legacy of the Holocaust. A lowering sky presides over the scene, which is illuminated by a hauntingly unnatural light. Both nature and the supernatural seem displaced by these icons of catastrophe.

The paintings of *In a Different Light* gather many questions, but offer few replies. They do not leave us groping in the dark, however, or launch us on a journey of mere aimless drifting. The angelic presence of *In that Direction** summons us to a new Armageddon of the future whose features remain undefined. Or perhaps it is reminding a forgetful Deity of the existence of the remnants of His creation on an abandoned rampart. Faces fly off like discarded discs: they will have to be redrawn to harmonize them with their role in the invisible landscape of human experience beyond the edge of the picture. Michelangelo had once painted the accepted boundaries of that adventure, which had been predetermined by the dictates of scriptural authority. Now the motif of meeting hands that had initiated the design has somehow gone awry. They seem to plead with the very title of the painting that depicts them: "in *which* direction?" The free-floating forearms are adrift, broken stone segments of a once unified self. But one officiating finger of real flesh proclaims its continuing survival while at the same time, perhaps – Bak's is a world of multiple possibilities – aiming an accusation against the absent Divinity. Such a charge would have been unthinkable to Michelangelo's majestic vision. The concentrated turmoil of *In that Direction* provides a stark critique for the modern era of that early Renaissance view.

* *page 69*

The motif of misplaced hands, a seminal metaphor of Bak's entire cycle, receives a more explicit reference in an eerie drawing in black and white crayon on blue paper ironically titled *In Good Hands*. An inverted image of Michelangelo's Adam at the instant of creation swirls into the distance. Imprinted on stone or canvas, Adam now dwells in a different dimension than the two angels before him, both powerless to establish contact with his essence. The artist as creator is vividly present through what we see; but God the Creator appears only through the nostalgia of memory. The hands of the drawing are linked by an invisible diagonal that bisects its design, their immobility fixed by the limitations of art. Their frozen gestures are far from the act of healing caress that truly "good" hands would use to restore vitality to those who were created in God's image. The ghostly pallor of *In Good Hands* is as distinct from the brilliant hues of *In that Direction* as a black and white film is from a Technicolor print. But the flurry of hands in both signi-

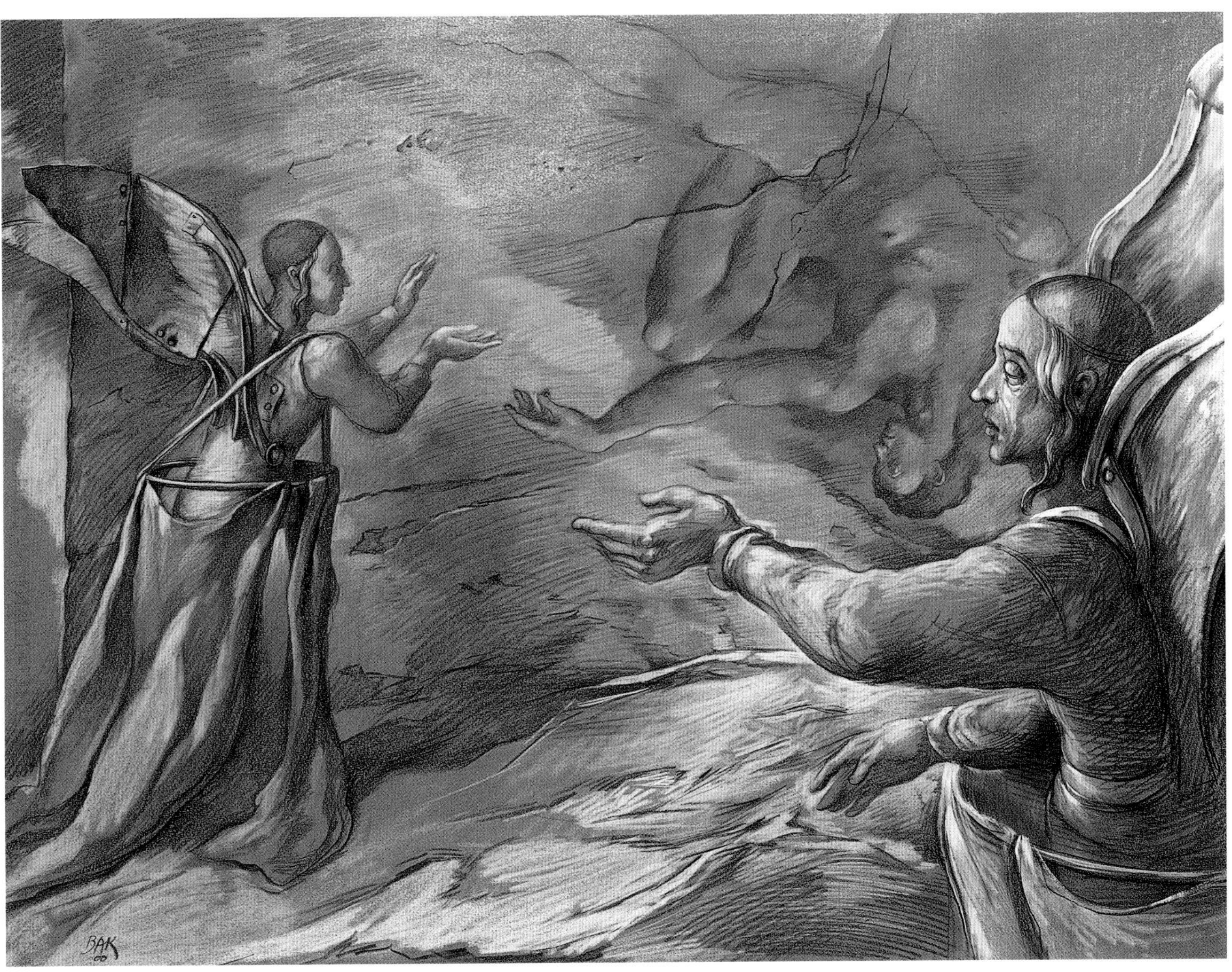

In Good Hands, 2000
Black & white crayon on blue/gray paper
19 3/4 x 25 1/2"

fies an ongoing search to mend the rupture or renew the contact between two worlds that once were mutually animated by the igniting touch between Adam and God. The art of Samuel Bak plays a vital role in reviewing the fate of that ancient metaphor in a post-Holocaust cosmos.

But memory is equally potent in the transaction between past and present. In Bak's paintings memory is divided between recollections of an ancient heritage whose controlling imagery was hierarchical and a modern legacy that questions the legitimacy of that vision, the one enshrined in the very architecture of the Sistine Chapel. In *Noah's Dream* the supine figure faces upward, the content of his nocturnal reverie floating above him. The momentum of ascent is reinforced by the vertical surge of the various biblical images that occupy the canvas. But two problems emerge that provoke inquiry. Genesis records no instance of Noah dreaming; Bak has invented his own version, perhaps interjecting some debris – sections of ladders - from Jacob's actual dream to prod the viewer to the challenge of interpretation, to ask whether we are dealing with prophecy and revelation, and if so, what each is meant to imply. The second problem is that this dream contradicts our expectations: it does not reflect the efflorescence of a restful sleep. Some of the images are familiar enough – the ark, the dove, the rainbow, the angels' wings – but they are hardly allowed to be reassuring. Among other memories evoked by Noah's story is the disenchanted benevolence behind God's promise never again to destroy His creation: "I will not again damn the soil on humankind's score. For the devisings of the human heart are evil from youth."[Gen. 8:21]If Noah was an exception, in Bak's rendering he resembles a weary modern traveler more than the last righteous man, "blameless in his time," who "walked with God." [Gen. 6:10] In Scripture Noah may have been God's chosen survivor, but in post-Holocaust history his counterpart's stamina will be seen by very few as a sign of divine blessing and protection. Noah's ark is now a painted image, and the curtain canvas that contains it shields our eyes from a more horrifying reality, one that the artist wisely chooses to leave to our imagination. The parallel ascents of Jacob's ladder to a hospitable heaven and the smoke from crematorium chimneys to a less friendly sky disturb the tranquility of Noah's repose, and for those of us aware of this dream's inner contradictions, its imagery converts it into the twisted incoherence of a nightmare. The witty inclusion of an umbrella and hat partially deflates the doleful legend of the deluge. But the blank canvas at Noah's feet that will greet him when he awakens is an earnest invitation to record modernity's version of

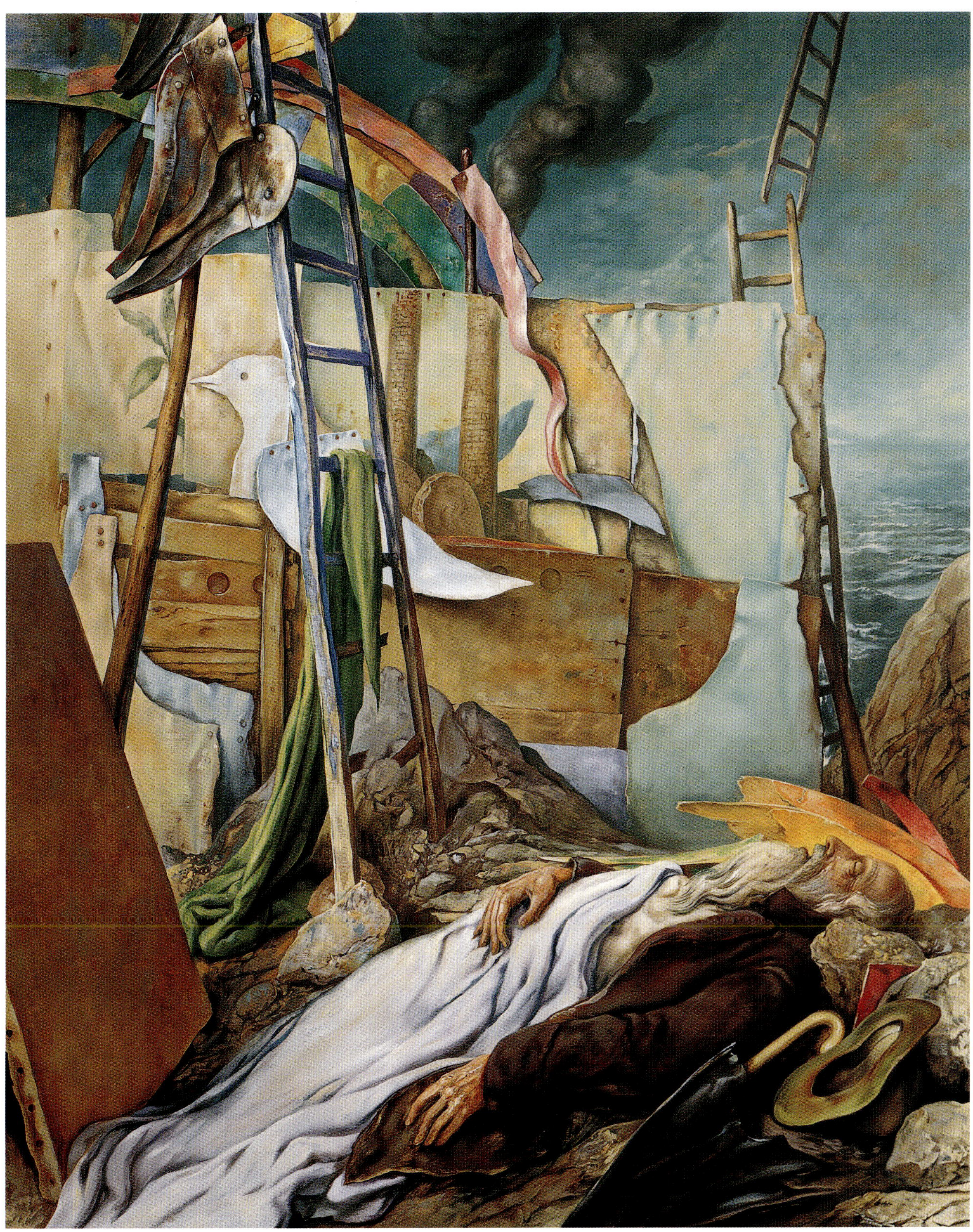

Noah's Dream, 1999
Oil on canvas, 40 x 32"

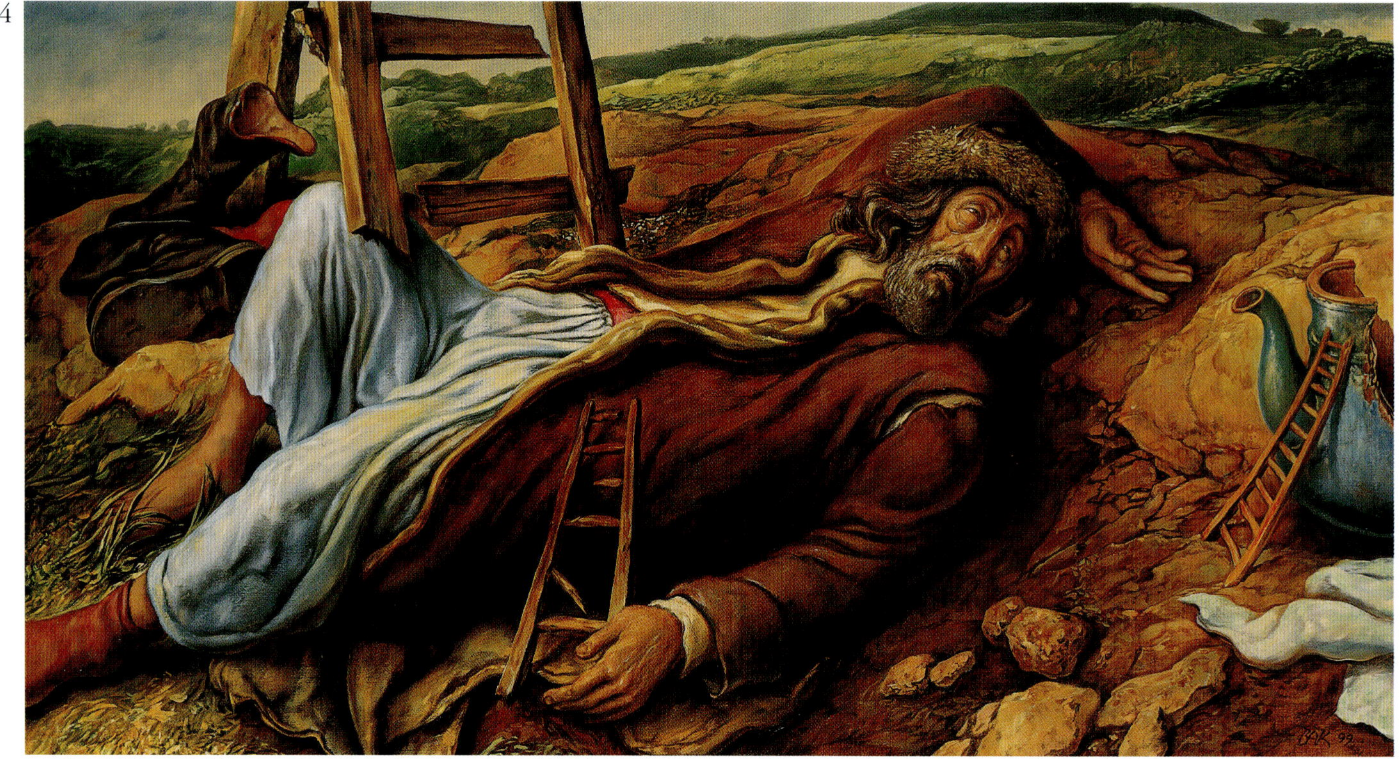

Sleepless Day, 1999
Oil on canvas, 16 x 30"

that event, though this time the element of destruction will be changed from water to fire.

Bedeviled by this dilemma, Bak in *Sleepless Day* transmutes the slumbering Jacob into a wakeful Chassidic Jew. In the absence of angels, he shares his solitude with a pair of miniature ladders and one larger replica that remains cropped and topless, climbing nowhere, on a landscape that offers a glimpse of horizon but virtually no sky. Here divine vistas are excluded, and his eyes are not turned upward, as we might expect of such a pious Jew, in a state of holy ecstasy. The former tokens of transcendence have shrunk to the size of toy structures or lost their capacity to soar. As divinely inspired dreams turn into secular nightmares, the melancholy Jew's aimless glance meets only a broken pitcher, a graphic image of the failed promise that haunts the memory of this devout scion of Jacob. What is he to make now of the ancient guarantee by the voice of God: "The land on which you lie, to you will I give it and to your seed"?

We are forced to focus instead on this heir of the patriarchs whose outstretched figure occupies the bulk of the canvas. His dispirited gaze is directed laterally, toward some earthly object. We are asked to imagine not what he sees, but what he remembers. For surely his eyes are turned inward, where memory engraves a scenario that is responsible for the expression of sad weariness on his face. It is as if the quasi-nightmare from which the Noah prototype will awaken keeps this contemporary Jew from sleep. Indeed, his insomnia is an antidote to amnesia, an unavoidable condition, perhaps, but a sign of exhaustion rather than repose. Is he pondering the loss of his co-religionists, reflecting on the fate of failed promises and shattered hopes, or is his trancelike demeanor merely a reflection of the overwhelming task before him: to remodel the spir-

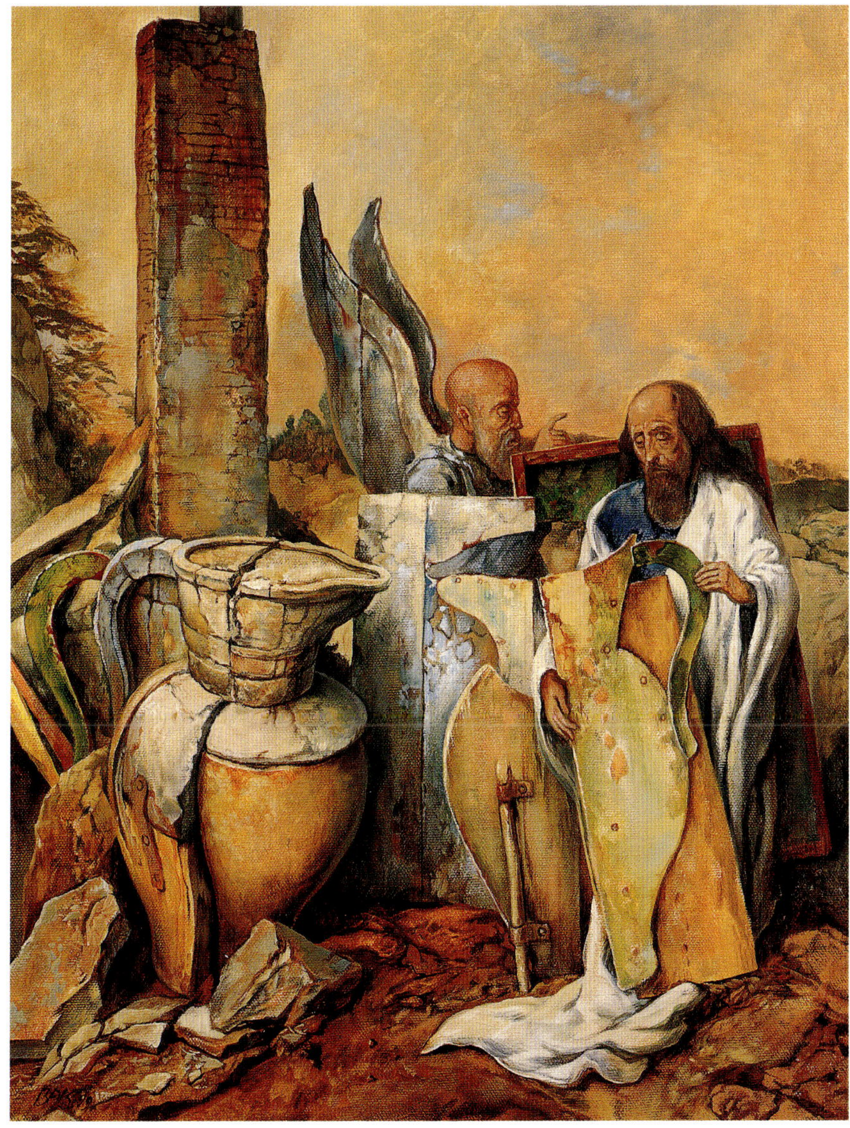

Restoring, 1999
Oil on canvas, 18 x 14"

itual reality that drives his being to include the debris of recent history, specifically the murder of European Jewry?

Two final paintings from *In a Different Light* may serve to illustrate Samuel Bak's artistic response to this enigma. After all, when the artist faces a blank canvas he or she must solve the issue of how to impose visual form on this void. In *Restoring**, an angel seems to be instructing a disciple on how to repair some pitchers damaged by an unknown catastrophe. The "pupil" holds a handle in the shape of a question mark, while other stone interrogatives wait their turn behind similar fragments. A framed painting separates the two figures, though its contents remain invisible. The angel's raised finger gathers a host of associations for the attentive viewer, but the true source of the problem draws only the spectator's attention, while the two figures disregard its presence. The looming chimney adjacent to the angel's wings concisely defines the requirements for a post-Holocaust vision of experience, but Bak leaves it to his audience to assemble its details. Creation is now a process of re-creation, a finding and renaming of parts, a willingness to forge an incoherent coherence from recent incongruities and to accept the resultant destabilized stability as an accurate reflection of the modern era. Nothing retains the equilibrium of its original conception, not even the once definitive version of Creation on the ceiling of the Sistine Chapel.

**page 75*

What then are we left with? In *Noah's Bird* Bak blends the twin disasters of flood and fire, providing a summary vision of how from biblical times to the present the good intentions of the creative urge have gone astray. Whether the source be divine anger or human evil, the debris-strewn landscape before us summons us to the ultimate moment of interpretation. The gentle dove from *Genesis*, no plucked olive leaf in its bill this time, stares at the surrounding terrain with a near-demonic intensity. The disquieting sight it beholds dares us to venture toward an even more distressing insight. Its terrifying gaze, the monstrosity of that mesmerizing eye, betrays far more than the mere ebbing of the waters, though it does not easily reveal the secret of what it sees. Is there a touch of madness to its allure, a schizoid split between innocent bird of peace and the anguish of the camp survivor whose striped garment threatens to consume the dove's original identity? The

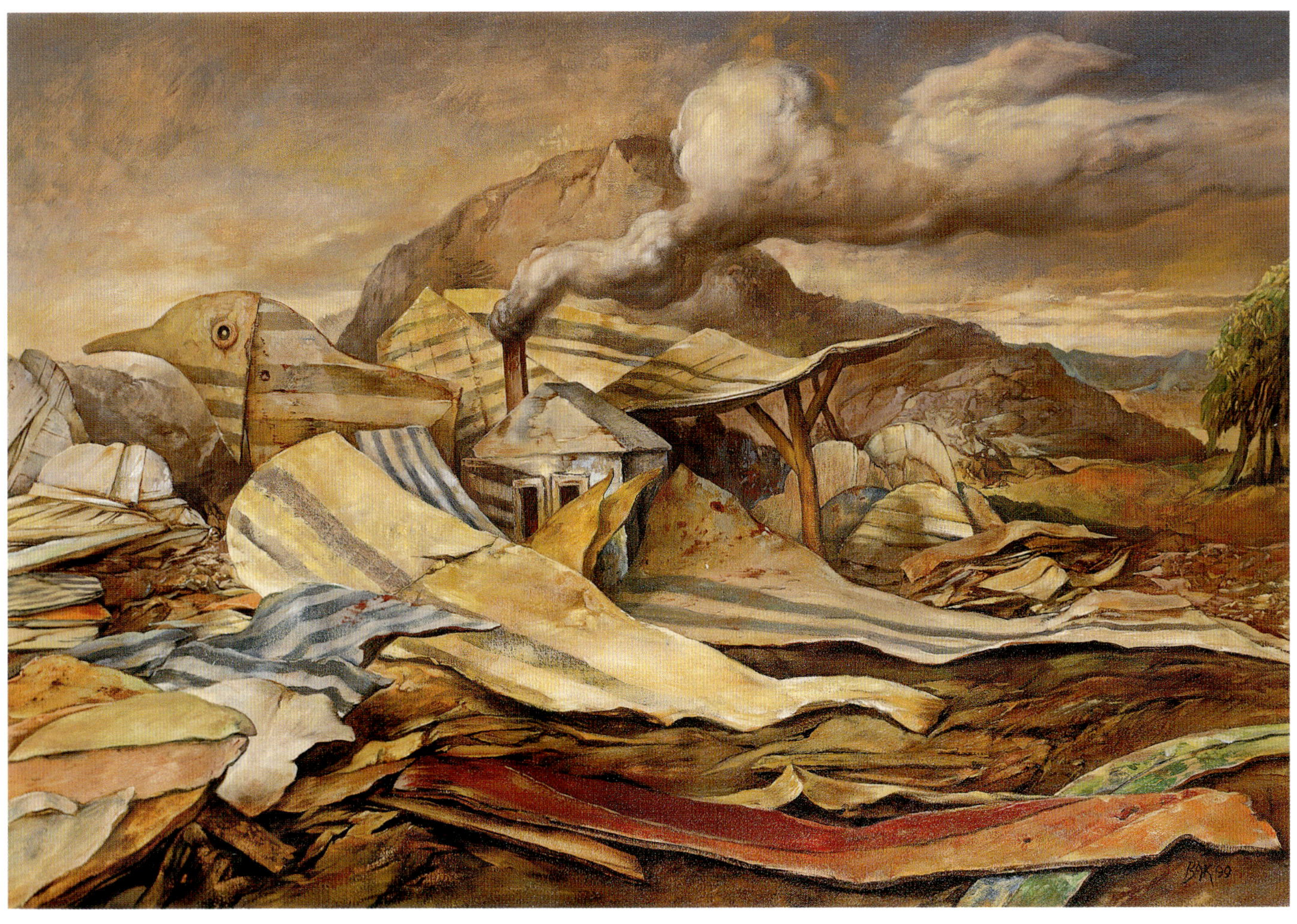

Noah's Bird, 1999
Oil on canvas, 20 x 30"

scraps of God's rainbow promise are scattered in the foreground, surrounded by vestiges of the same striped fabric that altered the integrity of the bird. How is it possible to reshape this detritus of history and scripture into a manageable – and even more important, a life sustaining – form? In the distance a mountain peak towers over the scene, but whether Sinai or Ararat, its barren summit offers no evidence of divine disclosure. Are we then faced with a return to anarchy, a more despondent version of T.S. Eliot's "Wasteland", whose fragments we are left with to shore against our ruin?

I do not think that the artist means to abandon us with this dismal prospect. Bak's most remarkable contribution to the evolution of a post-Holocaust sensibility is the tenacity with which he fashions through visual encounter a *point of view* for absorbing the intellectual and spiritual consequences of the destruction of

European Jewry. The atrocity that undid one version of Creation, evident in his blasted landscapes with their smoke-tainted skies, laid the foundations for a fresh way of seeing, one more sympathetic to the nature of modern reality. We might call it a principle of collateral perception, which then must grow slowly into a collateral mode of thought. It is an empirical rather than a theoretical process, spurring viewers to regard the tensions between biblical and historical narratives with a double vision that sustains simultaneously in a delicate inner balance the claims upon our imagination of creation and decay. They are engaged in perpetual strife, but the beguiling appeal of the paintings from *In a Different Light* to enter into their world of ambivalent duality prevents a victory for either side. At the original instant of creation God forced the darkness over the deep to recede to allow for the formation of our known cosmos, replacing the "waste and wild" of chaos with a human universe from which emerged the covenantal narrative of the Jewish people. Bak's cycle shows how through the Holocaust those ancient powers of discord have reasserted their primordial rights by trespassing on the world that displaced them. His art captures the resultant stress, leaving to his audience the chore of deciding how it affects or afflicts their consciousness and their lives.

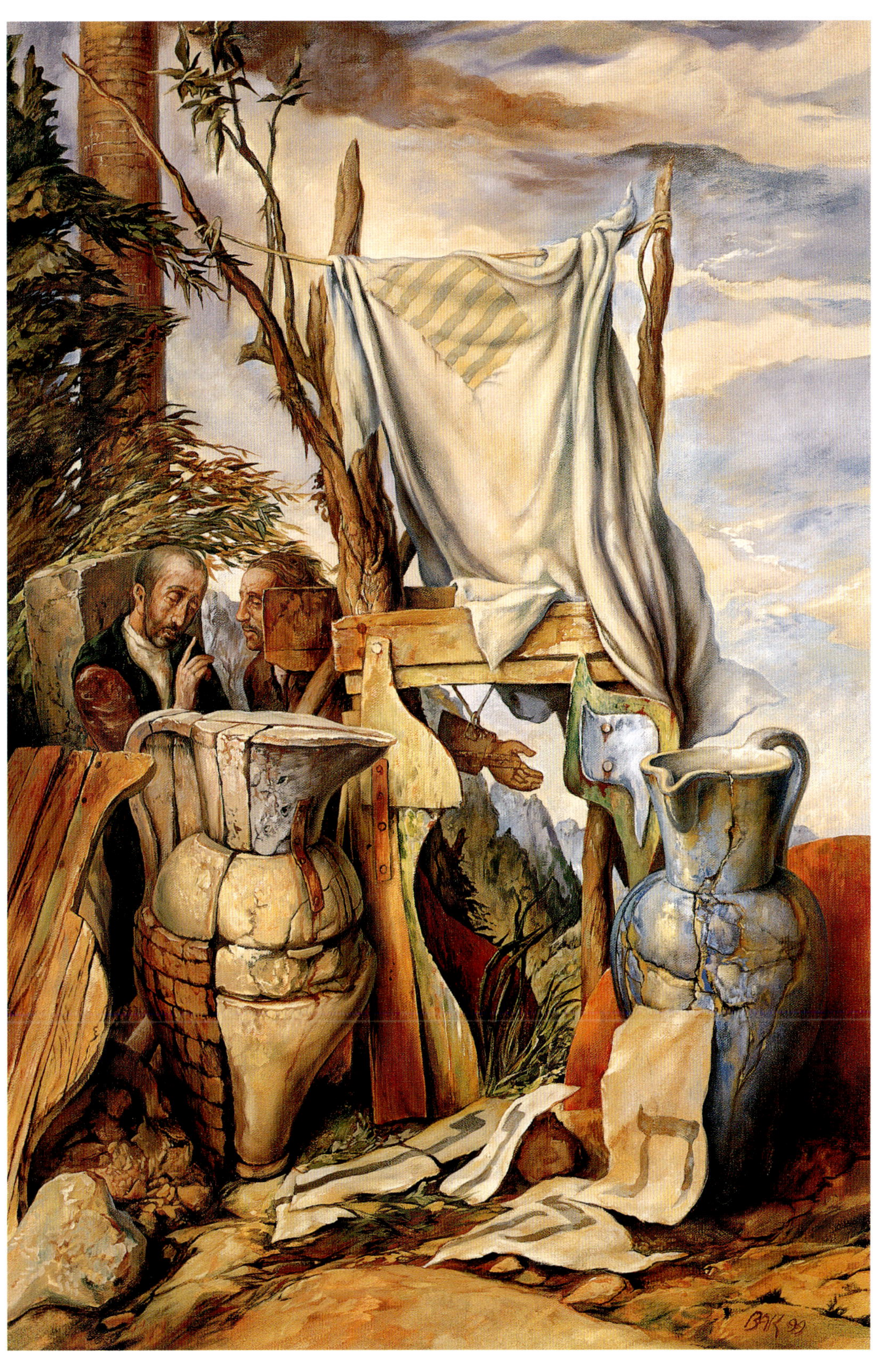

Sacred Debate, 1999
Oil on canvas, 30 x 20"

My Mother's *Bereyshiss**
by Samuel Bak

My studio is suffused with an odor of fresh varnish; the recent paintings lean against the studio walls and tables while their surfaces harden. In a few days they will be photographed, sent to the framer, brought to the gallery, and presented to the public. Again they are full of figures that look at me inquiringly: some in full form, some partially depicted, or merely suggested. Several have wings; others are constructed of decomposing stone. Rooted in the early chapters of the "Book of Genesis," many are based on familiar iconography, while others are purely personal inventions. Viewing the completed series releases in me a flood of thoughts. Between me and me, whenever I complete a series of new works, there arrives a moment of accounting.

As I contemplate the source of my move towards this Biblical material, I see two figures emerge from a large and dark space. They sit at a round table, sheltered under a huge silken lampshade that might well have been modeled on St. Peter's cupola in Rome. The lamp's bright yellow light bathes the table where an attractive woman spoon-feeds a boy of four, or five. He chews with ostentation and swallows very slowly. She talks to him intensely. His eyes are suspended on her lips.

"Lady," I feel like telling her, "this thing you are doing is absolutely wrong. A boy his age should be able to eat by himself. Believe me! I have raised three girls, and my grandson, now nine, ate by himself from a very early age." Something makes me keep my mouth shut. The little brat at the table is my own younger self.

"I would never have landed in these strange landscapes, had it not been for..." began my short introduction to the catalogue of my recent exhibition of chess-paintings. It was dedicated to the memory of my stepfather, whose deep devotion to the royal game, and tragic

**in yiddish: "In the Beginning" — GENESIS*

fading away from life, left me with a series of troubling images. Later these images generated scores of paintings and several exhibitions.

Speaking of my new paintings, I could use the same phrase again. *Had it not been for...* It was Mother's extraordinary gift for story-telling and the way she familiarized me with the tales of the "Book of 'Bereyshiss'" that landed me among these Biblical landscapes and inquiring figures.

I am always reluctant to define my work. I tend to say in public that my interpretations are no better than anyone else's, although in my heart I do think I know best. Yet experience has taught me that artists are not always their own best readers. All the same, what I can provide are some personal footnotes that may be of interest.

To me this present group of paintings is a post-Holocaust journey into the "Book of Genesis," and I would like to dedicate them to the lady under the huge lampshade: my personal "Papessa" (Italian for female Pope), my beloved, unique, bold, resolute, and often overbearing Mamma; in Polish, Mamousia; in plain Yiddish, Mameh.

My long-dead Mother never ceases to surprise me. How she knew to grab and cling to every straw during our days in the Ghetto, in hiding, and in the camps. How she struggled to keep us from going under. After having given me life on the day of my birth, she overcame the direst of circumstances to give me life again, and again. On the day of our liberation from the Nazis, we two were among the few hundred survivors of Vilna's eighty thousand Jews. Of course miracles paved our way, but they were miracles that called also for personal audacity and determination.

Recently Mother has been much on my mind. The few pages dedicated to my chess-paintings provoked in me an overwhelming flood of recollections. Whatever of my biography had not found its way onto my canvases – a healing process that spanned five decades – now began to fill the pages of an ever-swelling memoir.

I am plunged into my distant childhood, re-opening the gates of my private paradise and recording its loss. I bring back the endearing person of my father, gunned down at age thirty-seven. I summon generations of forebears – grandparents, aunts and uncles, all violently torn from the boy I was. They return to me with all their weaknesses, complexities, peculiarities, great capacity for love, and their unquestioning trust in my artistic calling.

It is a wonderful way to thank them, and say goodbye.

Towering over all these is Mother. She survived the Nazis and found resilience in her life in Israel, but a galloping cancer cut her down at age sixty. In my inner vision she repeatedly rejuvenates, ages, and is yet again restored to youth, according to the shifting waves of my recollection. I still mourn her too-early loss.

My writing owes a lot to my painting. In turn the memoir has greatly influenced what I now do at my easel. It has made me conscious of generations of forebears still alive in my mind and memory, and of yet earlier generations lost in the fogs of history. These distant ancestors alert me to an almost cosmic yearning, a desire to reach over the chasm of time and touch with my finger the moment of Adam's creation. Was it my awakened sense of ancestry that caused all this? I can't say. Yet something surely made me land in the arms of that bewildered couple, Adam and Eve – or is it perhaps that the mythological couple has landed in mine?

As I said, I owe to Mother my fascination with the stories of Genesis, or "Bereyshiss," as she used to call it. The magical tales about Adam, Noah, Abraham, Isaac, Jacob, and their respective spouses were handed out to me lovingly, together with a firm hand that would put into my mouth whatever was contained in a little silver spoon. It happened over numberless plates of sticky porridge; soups containing suspect and unidentifiable substances, scary to a child; slippery omelets with undercooked egg-whites; or hated vegetables. My forefathers had to see to it that I gained weight. We were in 1937 or 1938; the world smelt of oncoming war; distant thunder shook our walls.

"Eat my child, eat, and remember that before the fat man becomes thin, the thin one shall starve to death. Take a bite from this pear and you shall again hear the story of Paradise, and if you promise to finish all your lentil soup, I'll tell you about Jacob's stew." I loved the stories of my Biblical forefathers: dreamers, slave merchants, child-abusers, liars, betrayers, and even killers of brothers. How lucky I was to be an only child! Although these forebears baffled me, Mother taught me not to judge them. I would understand them better one day. Perhaps their troubling behavior was not entirely their fault, but how God made them. Only in much later generations, closer to my own time, did people greatly improve. Human redemption was possible. Mother was full of elevating stories about my four grandparents, loving and respectable citizens. But their stories could not compete with the fascination, drama, and magic of the heroic tales of the ancients, my great, great, great-grandfathers. The Patriarchs were in constant contact with God, with his angels, and with the challenging mystery of those times, and to me that made all the difference.

Maybe I should not undervalue the mystery of our own times. Once as a child trembling with fever on the floor of a small and overcrowded flat in the Vilna Ghetto, falling in and out of sleep, I suddenly saw a horned Moses caught among fluffs of dust under a dresser. He peeped at me from the glossy side of an old postcard from Rome, which depicted him beautifully sculpted in white marble. I understood the imploring look in his carved eyes, and cautiously relocated him from the dust into my pants pocket. Moses was another of my Biblical heroes, a leader who could have delivered us from Nazi slavery. But for me he performed a different service. In the Ghetto I was a child prodigy, a promising artist, but this Moses acquainted me with an even more promising artist, a certain Mr. Michelangelo. Mother explained that because his work was commissioned by a powerful Pope, he was able to do a lot of different projects. Knowing this, I sought out other reproductions of Mr. Michelangelo's art.

An old book provided me with some of what I sought. In one of the reproductions, a muscular young man, leaning languidly from the secure ground, reaches towards an older Moses-like figure, held aloft by scores of floating youngsters. The two men are pointing at each other in a most rude manner. Another engraving depicted a young and shapely couple, Adam and Eve. To the left they are seen on one side of a tree, with Adam reaching for the forbidden fruit, while on the other side we see the two of them, now aged and incredibly ugly, being banished from Paradise.

In the early 1960s I lived in Rome near the Sistine Chapel and could admire Michelangelo's original. It wasn't easy. The fresco was painted on a high, distant ceiling, and layers of ancient candle smoke covered its surface. Yet at the price of straining my neck and searching through powerful binoculars I could explore the painter's genius. Fortunately some Japanese TV money enabled the impoverished Church to pay for cleaning the "Creation." Later a smart editor made available a publication in which anyone can admire, at leisure and in total comfort, the electrifying colors of the Master's great art displayed on one's own coffee table.

Over the years, additional images of the Book of Genesis have been deposited in my mind. There is Doré's Bible, introduced to me by devoted Benedictine nuns who hid our family in the first months of the German Occupation. To a boy of seven or eight, the world of Doré looked frighteningly real. Older, I was captivated by Rembrandt's Biblical figures, which are taken from the daily reality of seventeenth-century Holland, examined with humility, and rendered with compassion. They go straight to the heart. In 1945 I discovered a lighter view of Genesis, first in Mark Twain's delightful "diary" of Adam and Eve, which I read in an old German translation shortly after arriving in the DP camp at Landsberg, Bavaria. I was twelve, and the idea that a sacred subject could be treated with humor was to me a revelation. I did not yet know the richness of Jewish humor, so familiar and beloved to me now: the "shtetl" patriarchs of Yitsik Manger's Yiddish poetry, or Chagall's whimsical, sad paintings. In another vein, the poetic translation of the Biblical texts into Yiddish, a monumental work by Yehoash, brought me closer to the original texts from which Mother's entrancing stories had been drawn.

Mother may be said to have extended my understanding of Genesis by taking me to Israel when I was fifteen. There I learned Hebrew, studied the Biblical texts in their original language, and with the help of the interpretations and commentaries of Rashi, Gordon, and many other luminaries, managed to savor the richness of every phrase in the Bible's immense text. I savored especially recovering in their own tongue those Patriarchs who were my great great great grandparents, on up to my four Grandparents and Father who were torn from me so violently and soon. Mother's entrancing tales of Genesis were still with me, but after the Holocaust they fell on different ears. Their essence was somehow darkened. At least for me, a post-Holocaust journey to Genesis must pass through the Book of Job. Job was one of the six million.

The many miracles that have punctuated my life – the miracle of my survival, of living in a free world where art has the right to exist, of my own fortunate career – all these have given the non-believer in me a strange feeling of awe, a feeling that benevolent angels have guarded me. Are there such angels? Do they still mediate between God and human beings, as in the time of Genesis? Can they understand the mysteries of our time?

The piteously man-made angels that populate my paintings do not pretend to represent such unearthly beings. My angels wear heavy wings of metal; they are spent and aged; their figures are composed of fragments; they are emanations of the inevitably constricted human imagination. At best they serve as Messengers among our varying human spheres of perception. I wonder whether these Angel Messengers can help us, or whether we don't encumber their ill-fitting wings by giving them impossible tasks. In my perpetual questioning I ask them to carry undecipherable messages from a God-fearing atheist to some superior presence, some silent voice from which like Job I seek adequate answers but receive none.

Does any of this explain the universe of my paintings? Certainly not! But I am lucky that a few enlightened Messengers, human yet well equipped with invisible wings, have taken on themselves the complex task of presenting and speaking about my art. They surely do it in a much better way than I ever would. The paintings that lean against the walls and tables have trust in their support – and so do I.

– Weston, March 2000

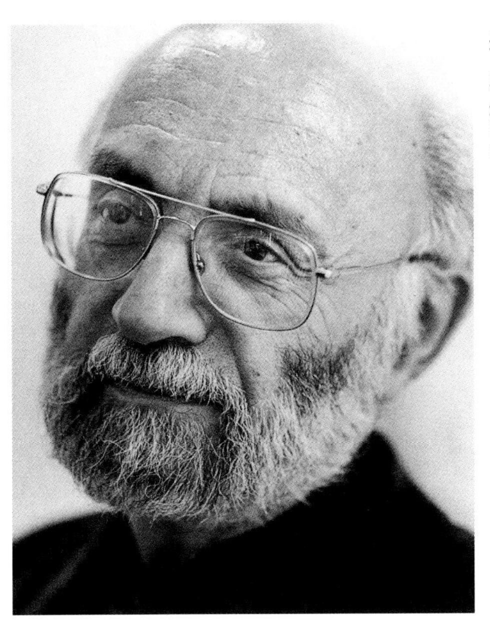

© Mikhail Lemkhin

Samuel Bak

1933	Born 12 August in Vilna, Poland.
1940–44	Under German occupation: ghetto, work-camp, refuge in a monastery.
1942	First exhibition of drawings in the ghetto Vilna.
1945–48	Displaced Persons camps in Germany; studied painting in Munich.
1948	Emigrated to Israel.
1952	Studied at the Bezalel Art School, Jerusalem.
1953–56	Army service.
1956	Received the First Prize of the American-Israeli Cultural Foundation.
1956–59	Lived in Paris. Studied at the "Ecole des Beaux-Arts."
1959–93	1959-66 lived in Rome; 1966-74 in Israel; 1974-77 in New York City; 1977-80 in Israel; 1980-84 in Paris; 1984-93 in Switzerland. 1993 Moved to Weston, Massachusetts.

Exhibitions & Restrospectives in Museums

Bezalel Museum, Jerusalem, Israel – 1963.
Tel Aviv Museum, Israel – 1963.
Brockton Art Center, Fuller Memorial, Brockton, Massachusetts – 1969.
SaidyE Bronfman Centre, Montreal, Canada – 1970.
Rose Museum, Brandeis, Waltham, Massachusetts – 1976.
Heidelberg Museum, Germany – 1977.
Kunstverein Esslingen, Germany – 1977.
Germanisches National Museum, Nuremberg, Germany – 1977.
Kunstmuseum, Dusseldorf, Germany –1978.
Rheinisches Landesmuseum, Bonn, Germany – 1978.
University of Haifa, Israel – 1978.
Museum Der Stadt, Landau, Germany – 1979.
Kunstmuseum, Wiesbaden, Germany – 1979.
Kunstverein Braunschweig, Germany – 1980.
Traveling Exhibition organized by Ministry of Culture and Education - visited 30 cultural centers in Israel – 1980-85.
Stadtgalerie Bamberg, Villa Dessauer, Germany – 1988.
"The Past Continues - Two Decades" **Koffler Gallery**, Toronto Ontario, Canada – 1990.
"The Past Continues" **Temple Judea Museum**, Philadelphia, Pennsylvania – 1991.
"Bak and Dürer" **Dürer Museum**, Nuremberg, Germany – 1991.
"Samuel Bak - Landschaften Jüdischer Erfahrung" **Jüdisches Museum**, Stadt Frankfurt am Main, Germany –1993
"Flight: Escape, Hope, Redemption" **Hebrew Union College** - Jewish Institute of Religion, New York, New York – 1994.
"Samuel Bak- A Retrospective Journey: Paintings 1946-1994" **Janice Charach Epstein Museum/Gallery**, West Bloomfield, Michigan – 1994.
"Myth, Midrash and Mysticism" **Spertus Museum**, Chicago, Illinois – 1995.
"Myth, Midrash, and Mysticism" **Mizel Museum of Judaica**, Denver, Colorado – 1995.
"Landscapes of Jewish Experience" **Wilshire Boulevard Temple**, Los Angeles, California – 1995.
"Myth, Midrash, and Mysticism" **The National Catholic Center For Holocaust Education**, Seton Hill College, Greensburg, Pennsylvania – 1995.
"Myth, Midrash, and Mysticism" **Rosen Museum Gallery**, Boca Raton, Florida – 1996.
"The Landscape of Jewish Experience" **Holocaust Museum Houston**, Texas – 1997.
"The Landscape of Jewish Experience" **B'nai B'rith Klutznick National Jewish Museum**, Washington, D.C. – 1997.
"Angels From Elsewhere" **Phillips Exeter Academy**, Exeter, New Hampshire – 1997.
Susquehanna University, Selinsgrove, Pennsylvania – 1998.
Panorama Museum, Bad Frankenhausen, Germany – 1998.
"Transformation and Transfiguration", **Snite Art Museum**, Notre Dame, Indiana – 2000
"Samuel Bak: Working Through The Past", **Florida Holocaust Museum**, St. Petersburg, Florida – 2001

Solo Gallery Exhibitions

Galleria Schneider – 1959, 1961, 1965, 1966
Galleria Liguria – 1963.
L'Angle Aigu, Brussels – 1965.
Alwin Gallery, London – 1965.
Gordon Gallery, Tel Aviv – 1966.
Roma Gallery, Chicago – 1967.
Modern Art Gallery, Jaffa – 1968.
Pucker Safrai Gallery, Boston –
1969, 1972, 1975, 1979,
1985,1987, 1989, 1991.
Hadassah "K" Gallery, Tel Aviv – 1971, 1973, 1978.
Aberbach Fine Art, New York – 1974, 1975, 1978.
Ketterer Gallery, Munich – 1977.
Amstutz Gallery, Zurich – 1978.
Vonderbank Gallery, Frankfurt – 1978.
Goldman Gallery, Haifa – 1978.
DeBel Gallery, Jerusalem – 1978, 1980.
Galerie Levy, Hamburg – 1980.
Thorens Fine Art, Basel – 1981.
Kallenbach Fine Art, Munich – 1981, 1983, 1984, 1987.
Soufer Gallery, New York – 1986, 1988, 1990, 1992.
Galerie Ludwig Lange, Berlin – 1987.
Galerie Carpentier, Paris – 1988.
Galerie M.A.G., Paris – 1989.
Galerie Marc Richard, Zurich – 1990.
Galerie de la Cathedrale, Fribourg – 1991, 1992.
Galerie Picpus, Montreux – 1991, 1992.
Pucker Gallery, Boston – 1993.
"Landscapes of Jewish Experience"
Pucker Gallery, Boston – 1995.
"The Fruit of Knowledge"
Pucker Gallery, Boston – 1996.
"Landscapes of Jewish Experience II"
George Krevsky Fine Art, San Francisco, CA – 1998.
Pucker Gallery, Boston – 1998. "In the Presence of Figures"
Pucker Gallery, Boston – 2000. "The Game Continues"
Pucker Gallery, Boston – 2000. "In A Different Light"

Selected Group Exhibitions

The Carnegie International, Pittsburgh – 1961.
"Image and Imagination", Tel Aviv Museum – 1967.
"Jewish Experience in the Art of the 20th Century," Jewish Museum, New York – 1975.
International Art Fair, Basel – 1979, 1981, 1982, 1984, 1986.
"Nachbilder," Kunstahalle, Hannover – 1979.
"Bilder Sind Nicht Verboten," Stadtische Kunstahalle, Düsseldorf – 1982.
"Still Life," Tel Aviv Museum – 1984.
International Art Fair, Ghent – 1986.
"Chagall to Kitaj", Barbican Art Center, London – 1990.
"Witness and Legacy", Travelling Group Exhibition in North America – 1995 - present.

Public Collections

Boston Public Library, Boston, MA
DeCordova Museum, Lincoln, MA
Dürer House, Nuremberg, Germany
Frances Lehman Loeb Art Center, Vassar College, Poughkeepsie, NY
Germanisches National Museum, Nuremberg, Germany
German Parliament, Bonn, Germany
Hobart & William Smith College, Geneva, NY
Holocaust Museum Houston, Houston, TX
Hood Museum, Dartmouth College, Hanover, NH
Imperial War Museum, London, UK
Israel Museum, Jerusalem, Israel
Jewish Museum, New York, NY
Jüdisches Museum, Stadt Frankfurt am Main, Germany
Kunstmuseum, Bamberg, Germany
Municipality of Nuremberg, Germany
National Gallery of Canada, Ottawa, Ontario, Canada
National Museum, Vilnius, Lithuania
Panorama Museum, Bad Frankenhausen, Germany
Phillips Exeter Academy, Exeter, NH
Rose Museum, Brandeis, Waltham, MA
University of Haifa, Israel
Tel Aviv Museum of Art, Tel Aviv, Israel
Yad Vashem Museum, Jerusalem, Israel
Vaud State, Switzerland.

Monographs/Books

Chess as Metaphor In the Art of Samuel Bak, Jean Louis Cornuz. Boston & Montreux, 1991.
Samuel Bak, The Past Continues, Samuel Bak and Paul T. Nagano. David R. Godine, Boston, 1988.
Bak, Monuments to Our Dreams, Rolf Kallenbach. Limes Verlag, Weisbaden & Munich, 1977.
Bak, Paintings of the Last Decade, A. Kaufman and Paul T. Nagano. Aberbach, New York, 1974.
Ewiges Licht (Landsberg: A Memoir 1944-1948), Samuel Bak. Jewish Museum Frankfurt, 1996.
Landscapes of Jewish Experience, Lawrence Langer. University Press of New England, 1997.
Samuel Bak Retrospektive 1946-1997, Panorama Museum - Bad Frankenhausen, 1998.
The Game Continues, Lawrence Langer. Pucker Art and Indiana University Press, 1999.

List of Paintings

Lawrence L. Langer

Lawrence L. Langer was born in New York City and educated at City College of New York and Harvard University. He is Alumnae Chair Professor of English Emeritus at Simmons College in Boston. His books include The Holocaust and The Literary Imagination (1975), The Age of Atrocity: Death in Modern Literature (1978), Versions of Survival: The Holocaust and Human Spirit (1982), Holocaust Testimonies: The Ruins of Memory (1991), which won the National Book Critics Circle Award for Criticism and was named one of the ten best books of the year by the editors of the New York Times Sunday Book Review. Admitting the Holocaust: Collected Essays (1995), Art from the Ashes: A Holocaust Anthology (1995), Landscapes of Jewish Experience: Paintings by Samuel Bak (1997), for which he wrote the text and critical commentaries, and Preempting the Holocaust (1998).